PRAISE FOR

Creativity

"Like all extraordinary artists, Philippe Petit's practice is founded in rigor, scrutiny, and dedication. What sets Philippe in a class all his own is his restless quest to conquer the greatest physical heights, achieving a precise balance of chaos and creativity. He is an inspiration to all who dare to dream of the seemingly impossible. Dear friend: I salute you!"

—Mikhail Baryshnikov

"A book as unique, open, and inspiring as one would expect from its fundamentally revolutionary creator, a true original who does not accept accepted wisdom or take no for an answer. As I read, I kept underlining and thinking of friends I wanted to share it with—actors, writers, directors, anyone, really. This book could be as powerful for kids as adults; I put a copy of it on each of my kids' nightstands, and recommend you do the same."

—David Duchovny

"If life itself is a walk on a wire, suspended between birth and death, in *Creativity: The Perfect Crime* Philippe Petit reminds us that the humble precision of every little step can lead to greatness." —Francesco Clemente

"I enjoyed the organization of chaos, the boldness of ideas, the insanity of Philippe's visions, the extreme discipline of planning, and the passion of the feat. It inspires to create not only on a sound concept, but also on a whim or a spark. I was thoroughly able to identify with his highs and lows and it was a great pleasure to have one so freewheeling put his methods down in a completely personal way."

—Julie Taymor

"Philippe Petit created one of the greatest works of art of the twentieth century. He is also a most intelligent and original thinker (not to mention terrific company). How lucky we are to have him as a guide into the elusive and all-important subject of creativity."

—Jonathan Safran Foer

Creativity

The Perfect Crime

Philippe Petit

Illustrated by the author

Riverhead Books
New York

Creativity takes courage.

—HENRI MATISSE

To Evelyne Crochet, an exceptional pianist and monumental friend.

Whether I write or walk the wire, your interpretations of Bach,
Satie or Schubert keep me on the creative line;
you possess that ever-so-rare blend
of command and self-effacement, daring and moderation,
with depth of insight, that makes a master artist.

Along with those of Buster Keaton, Señor Wences, Francis Brunn,
Marlon Brando and Werner Herzog, your portrait (at Carnegie Hall)
hangs inside the barn where I practice daily.

Your distinctive creativity, guided by poetry, tenacity
and perfection, has long served as model to me.

You inspire much more than this book.

CREATIVITY

(pronounced *ch'ien*)

 This symbol represents a time when creativity brings success. It is the first hexagram in the four-thousand-year-old book of philosophy *I Ching: The Book of Changes.*

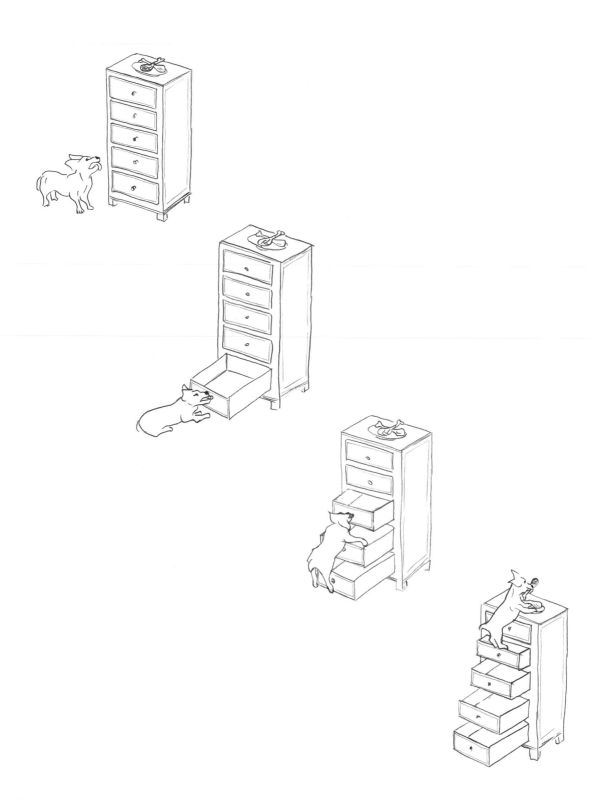

Contents

A FORETHOUGHT

Confession of an Outlaw

Make no mistake.

I frown upon books about creativity.

Too often they gather only formulas, point at Einstein and the Beatles but rarely at the author, propose exercises that mistake the mind for a gym machine and conclude each chapter with a recap worthy of fifth-graders. In aiming at the universal—to satisfy the commonest denominator of human thinking and behavior—most of these books miss all of the originality, the humor, the serendipity, the grace, the exceptions to the rule, the idiosyncrasies that mold the way of art.

So if I don't believe in books about creativity, why am I writing one?

Although the original idea for this book was not mine—it came from the outside—its entire content comes directly from inside, from a life I have spent creating. I hope that my unconventional, insubordinate process of creativity will offer insight for anyone struggling to achieve his or her dreams.

Born into the confines of rigid parenting, repressive schooling and the narrow-mindedness of a country busy manufacturing 365 types of cheeses, quite early I started to rebel against authority. I was not very good at following. I had to distance myself from the norm, to venture along solitary paths, to teach myself.

At six, I taught myself magic; at fourteen, juggling; at sixteen, wire-walking. In the process, I was thrown out of five different schools. Regardless, I would never have let my schooling get in the way of my education.

Observation was my conduit to knowledge, intuition my source of power. I spent my days taking things apart and rebuilding them; not asking how to do something, but finding out; hiding from people in order to stare at them, noting how they dress, talk, act, and noticing their mistakes . . .

As a teenager I spent considerable time at the circus and vaudeville theater, witnessing the best acts in the world—thereby setting my artistic standards at an unusually high level. I would compare the overall effect different performances had on me and decide who was the best dancer, the best ventriloquist, the best stand-up comic. I would try on their styles and attempt their routines. Ha-ha! Yet trial and error provided results.

All of this trying and failing and watching and trying again bred in me an arrogant, proud and aggressive determination. Each discovery, no matter how naive, had to be jealously hidden from the rest of the world. Each victory felt like a stolen jewel. I fell into a natural state of intellectual self-defense. Let me explain.

Always trying my best, I became guilty of pursuing perfection—imagine that!

Always working relentlessly, I became obstinate—and almost felt guilty about it.

To protect what triggered my creativity, I became secretive.

Anxious about being discovered, fearful of being caught, I ended up always on the lookout.

At the outset of most projects, busy battling against overwhelming odds, I came to believe the entire world was against me.

This was a reflection of reality as well as the frame of mind I needed to be at my most creative. It coated my character with an outlaw sheen. And I'm sure that with my constant sneaking, my tiptoeing, my way of approaching people inconspicuously from behind to spy on them or surprise them, I must have looked like a criminal, and certainly others must have felt I was one. And so I was not surprised the world around me reacted with suspicion and mistrust!

Before I had reached eighteen, I had rewritten the Book of Ethics that had been forced on me earlier, and before I knew it, I had acquired the mind of a criminal.

My attitude as an artist grew out of the realization I'd arrived at from an early age: that my intellectual engagement, my imaginative freedom, had a price, that of the forbidden. Whatever I decided to do, it was not allowed! "Creativity is illegal" became my byword.

The creator must be an outlaw.

Not a criminal outlaw, but rather a poet who cultivates intellectual rebellion. The difference between a bank job and an illegal high-wire walk is paramount: the aerial crossing does not steal anything; it offers an ephemeral gift, one that delights and inspires.

Despite my outlaw approach—or because of it—a network of personal creative principles imperceptibly emerged. Lawlessness doesn't mean lack of method: in fact, the outlaw I became needed method all the more, because I was swimming alone to the island of my dreams.

With the urgency of those who believe life is short, I found multiple ways of getting things done, I solved problems intuitively, and by refusing failure, I was able to achieve the impossible.

I dedicated myself to my arts, bringing to bear a fanatic attention to detail and little respect for the established values of competition, money or social status.

For my first major high-wire walks—at Notre Dame, the Sydney Harbor Bridge and the World Trade Center—*Oops!*—I forgot to ask permission. And after, I certainly did not seek forgiveness.

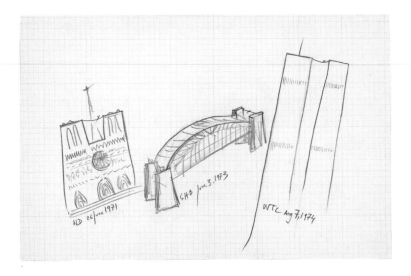

Over the years, I went on refining a highly personal creative process. I kept drawing on my autodidactic elasticity, all the time knowing that I was never alone in my progress: mentors, friends and illustrious artists in a wide range of creative fields guided me and opened doors. They were masters of one craft, however, and I was . . . a defiant Renaissance Boy wanting to do it all!

One day I was asked to share my creative process with others in the form of a lecture. I concocted a lively mixture of physical demonstrations, experiments with props, audience participation, storytelling, live drawings, quizzes and even magic tricks; and I took pleasure in revealing some of my creative secrets.

Word of my lectures spread and I was encouraged to do more.

My audience grew to be quite diverse: aspiring wire-walkers, Nobel Prize winners, clergymen; millionaires whose focus lacked focus and businessmen striving to become millionaires; young entrepreneurs, people seeking a direction in life, curious souls, and students of all sorts of subjects.

My audiences seemed to identify with my outlaw attitude, to be inspired by my propensity for venturing far off the beaten path. They asked me to elaborate on my "grammar of creativity," and even the tech geeks I spoke to were hungry for more of this self-confessed Luddite's primer on self-teaching and self-discovery.

Eventually I distilled my audience's favorite topics into a one-man show, *WIRELESS! Philippe Petit Down to Earth*. And I began to see that despite my aversion to guides to the creative process, I really did have the makings of a book.

But not a book about creativity.

A book about *my* creativity.

So think of this book as a conspiracy—or, if you will, a manifesto. And think of yourself, dear reader, as an accomplice who is invited to explore your own field of intellectual or artistic "crime."

See this book not as a blueprint for any specific crime but as a series of postcards from the labyrinths I build (to confuse those chasing me), the tunnels I dig (to escape), the dams I erect (to delay the invasion of the elements). Accept my invitation to become my student, my partner, in crime. Together we'll take chances and yet leave nothing to chance. We'll question the questions, yet arrive at definitive principles. We'll be stubbornly focused, yet curious about everything.

I hope this book will provide guidance for your imagination. That it will help you to recognize all sorts of obstacles, in order to circumvent them, or— if need be—make them vanish. That it will reveal to you the surest way to bring your "criminal intentions" from inspiration to full-fledged execution— to "coup." And that along the way, it imparts what I have discovered about the benefits of passion, tenacity, intuition, misdirection, daily practice, secrets, mistakes, surprises and believing in miracles.

Most of all, I fervently wish it will remind you of the qualities hidden inside all of us, that we are rarely encouraged to recognize but that are essential to make our dreams come true, to plan, design and construct a wondrous life.

I wish you the most adventurous journey, epic pursuit and successful escape.

Vehemently yours,

PHILIPPE PETIT
10 Rue Laplace, Paris
October 6, 2012*

---

*Usually the preface bears the date of the finished manuscript, not its commencement—as the author of a book on creativity, I'm happy to break that rule.

((((((((Blue? You want blue?   ))))))))

True, red is ambitious and bragging; it is evocative of fire, love, blood and inferno—it stops our car at a crossing. Green has a clean and natural skin; it signals "You may go"—but some feel it is unstable and shouldn't be trusted. Yellow has often represented the foreign, the distant, has been tainted by infamy, yet it carries power and longevity—for centuries in China it was reserved for the emperor.

But blue, as the sky, as the sea—blue tries to be official when it tints uniforms, yet it mingles commonly as it colors jeans. So limpid and tranquil blue it is.

Therefore, in the body of each chapter, you will encounter a word or expression printed in **blue**. It invites you to jump to the end of the chapter, where a little digression patiently awaits, printed all in blue.

((((((((((((((•))))))))))))))

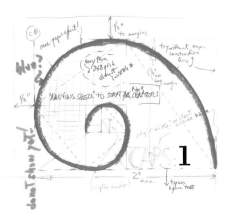

1 THE BLANK PAGE

I see the page on the right.

It is blank.

If I turn back the page and this time *look*, the page will still be blank, but it will offer additional impressions.

Looking draws me into observing.

I observe: I explore.

Each exploring step leaves a trace on the territory I claim as I progress.

I explore: I conquer.

The cliché of the anxious writer, pen frozen above a blank first page, never occurs to me. Instead, the blank page triggers wild anticipation. I'm on the edge of my seat, like an impatient child.

Please follow me.

Invitation

With wondrous generosity, the blank page invites me . . .

I am the graphic designer who divides space, who decides where to place text and illustrations in a meaningful and harmonious way, who already day-dreams about **the printing miracle** ahead.

I am the self-taught writer with polyglot passion who scribes down little signs called letters, who groups them into words, gathers them into sentences, forms paragraphs—enough to fill the opening of my yet-to-be-authored first novel . . . or is it my groundbreaking engineering theory . . . or, why not, my definitive translation from Russian of Vladimir Vysotsky's "Challenging Horses" (the song Mikhail Baryshnikov dances to in an empty Bolshoi Theater in the film *White Nights*).

I am the professional daydreamer who surrenders to the automatic wandering of his pen and covers the page with meaningless doodles, then turns them into recognizable shapes: animals, caricatures, monsters, castles in the sky.

I am the frustrated movie director (my first film still inside my head) who draws a grid and fills each frame with rough-sketched action before he decides if the completed storyboard is a motion picture ready to be shot.

I am the lecturer focused on problem-solving who holds in my left hand a piece of paper and in my right a three-dimensional paper construction, and challenges the audience: "Can you make *this* . . . into *that* . . . without adding and gluing?"—and who then proceeds to demonstrate how the seemingly impossible feat can be done in three seconds if you relinquish one-dimensional thinking.

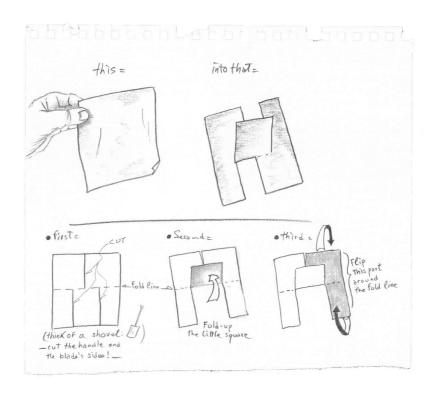

I am the Mischief-Master I've always been (that is, Lippo, my silent street-juggling character of forty-five years), who breaks the rules by tearing the page into three strips, crumbles each into a ball and juggles them! No, the pieces are too small and too light, the breeze too strong—the performance won't last beyond the initial "One-two-three" exchange (but certainly dedicated practice can change that).

I am the rogue engineer who folds the blank sheet into a paper plane, sends it into the sky and watches it disappear in the clouds or land softly at the feet of a child.

I am the Master of Deception—the illusionist performing close-up magic for nearly sixty years—who *walks through the page!* A tour de force? Yes and no. If you are good with sharp scissors and supple-limbed, it's easy. You just have to know the exact cuts required.

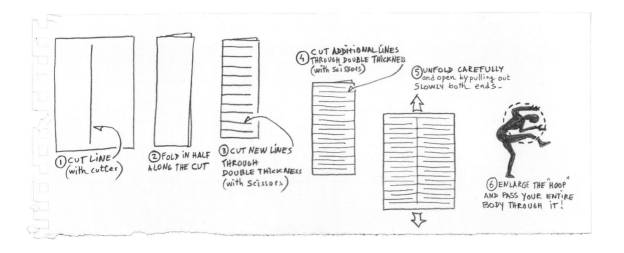

I am the passionate drawing-artist I've always been, who suspends his charcoal for a moment above the large blank sheet of Fabriano before he traces lines and adds values that reveal a grand canyon at dusk with a high wire ready to be walked on and a sky of overlapping shades and shapes, portrait of an angry storm.

Did I see the paper stock only as a surface? Or did I remember my private lessons with master pastellist Sam Szafran, who shared with me his method of feeding the paper with graphite: "Assault the paper. It is thick, draw with depth. Scratch the sheet, with a nail, with a coin; make the pigment penetrate the layers. Erase, then draw again. Fatigue the paper; erode its skin. Erase, then draw again."

As I force the drawing to emerge from the thick white sheet, I remember what is said about Michelangelo. The perfect sculpture of a rearing horse is hidden inside the block of marble the artist faces. Only after he has found the creature and admired its form can he begin to extract it, unscathed— to free it, one chisel blow at a time.

Finding the horse is hard art, I think; sculpting it is . . . just hard work.

Regardless of what I do with the blank page—what I give to it or steal from it; whether I abuse it, hijack it or free it, consider it flat or give it volume, send it flying to heaven or to hell—I affix to it a hint of my mood, a trait of my character, a morsel of my existence, a part of me.

Like Picasso (who by hand added *Je suis le* above the printed word CAHIER on his sketchbook cover), I declare: *Je suis la page.* I am the page.

And what about you? How do you respond to the blank page? How does the blank page respond to you? *Are you the page?*

A book of white

Oh, I forgot one option.

What about doing nothing, just facing the blank page? As an expression of ultimate serenity, highest wisdom.

That I cannot imagine. For me, inaction in the face of the blank page is not an option. Or if it occurs, it will not be because I don't know what to do, but rather the opposite: I've got a million solutions to choose from!

I know I'll never be the Tibetan monk seated in lotus position who contemplates a pile of blank pages set on the terrace of his Himalayan monastery.

But wait!

That image conjures back the aspiring filmmaker. I am the director and I want to try something!

I ask my actor to throw the stack high in the air, where an icy breeze steals the pages and sends them tumbling one by one, like sacred kites, toward the faraway white peaks . . .

"Cut!"

Let's rewind in slow motion, until all the sheets are back, neatly stacked on the terrace.

Ah . . . a stack of blank pages! How appealing!

Glued, stapled or sewn, trimmed and bound, they become a book of white— what publishers call a dummy.

Fill it with printed words, and it's a book to read!

Passionately yours

If you think that I am now going to tell you how I am motivated to fill blank pages, you are wrong.

There is no such thing as motivation in my world. I am not *motivated* to do what I do. As an artist, I am driven, I am compelled, I am thrust forward by a force so rooted inside me, so convincing, that it seems futile to try to explain it. Although it has a name: passion.

Passion is the mortar that holds my creative assemblies together. It is the motor of my actions. Because it is in perpetual motion, it has an impatient edge to it. It is urgent. And because it invites my arts to grow, it is essential.

Propelled by such winds of passion, for whom do I create? Do I perform for myself or for an audience?

My answer sits on both sides of that boundary.

When I am in the park, juggling inside my circle of chalk, I need to intrigue the passersby or else they will keep moving. During the performance, my comic character Lippo, who feeds on the crowd, reads the audience, ready to take advantage of their slightest reaction. And the instant I sense a hint of lethargy hovering above the crowd, I'll interrupt my juggling and launch a *coup de théâtre* sure to wake up everyone—I'll blow my whistle and set a tightrope between two trees!

At the same time, in order to offer the most honest performance, I must be all alone. I must be prisoner of the fortress of my art.

The true artistic impulse has nothing to do with pleasing the audience—or, for that matter, with pleasing the impresario so you'll get more jobs or more money. That's not art. If you are an artist, you want to create a giant wall around yourself and, inside that wall, to follow your honesty and your intuition. What the audience will see is a man or woman who is prisoner of his or her passion, and that is the most inspiring performance in the world.

So there you have it, an answer full of contradictions: I have a subtle disregard for the audience, for whom I have the utmost attention and regard!

And that brings us near my beloved Fields of Contradictions, which I'll invite you to explore with me soon enough.

In the meantime, what should you be passionate about?

Let's start there.

((((((((the printing miracle))))))))

When I was thirteen, my curiosity for the graphic arts landed me an apprenticeship on Thursdays (at the time a day off from school in France) at Les Imprimeries de la Drôme et du Verdon, a reputable Parisian printing plant. I learned to set type by hand and to use the giant press, which had not progressed much since Gutenberg's era.

For hours I strained my left wrist to maintain a little rack, the *composing stick*, in the correct yet utterly unnatural position. In the tray before me, *la casse*, I found capital letters at the top—thus *haut-de-casse* (uppercase) and *bas-de-casse* (lowercase) letters at the bottom. For each line of text, I had to place on the stick the metal characters (mirror images of letters, in relief) one by one upside down and running from right to left.

When I finished composing a line, I placed it on a little zinc tray representing one page. And when my tray was full, I carefully transferred its contents to a bottomless frame, tightly imprisoning all its parts with steel expansion clamps. If I left any clamp a trifle loose, the entire work would shatter into hundreds of pieces all over the floor, to the amusement of the professionals around me.

Although the repeated act of fishing tiny characters from the brimming *casse* brought tears to my eyes, I grew to appreciate that the result should not form a group of beautiful letters, but a beautiful group of letters.

I became expert at recognizing fonts. Some had serifs—hairlines that extend their limbs elegantly and ease the reading. The limbs of the sans serif family, by contrast, ended abruptly, yet proved more practical for certain compositions.

Being surrounded by letters, I quite naturally invented my own font and proudly employed it to send my pals handwritten missives that proved hard to decipher.

At the end of the day, after the professional typesetters had finished their work, there was a short time when I was allowed to use the press before it was shut down for the night. Under close supervision, I placed my composed frames on the bed of the giant machine and set it in motion.

Seconds later, the magic of printing revealed itself, and I was all smiles until I read what had been printed on the coarse sheet (I was not allowed to waste good stock). There, in all their indelibility, were my many typographic errors. And yet, how proud I was!

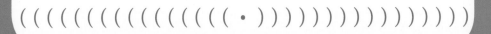

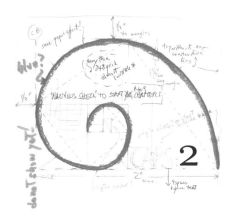

2 CHAOS & ORDER

Passion is explosive.

It knows no bounds.

It can't be measured.

I let it boil over—to the point that sometimes I think and talk in all directions.

Do you speak to yourself? I often do (silently).

In keeping with our outlaw enterprise, why don't you eavesdrop on me as I interview myself?

The gallop of Chaos

So, how does the outlaw artist go about embarking on the "perfect crime"? What's the first step? What's the recipe?

There is no recipe.

Okay. What is the first step?

My first step?

Chaos.

That's how I set my artistic crimes in motion.

I toy with an idea until it becomes a fixation. The French have a name for it: *idée fixe*. It is an idea that you lodge in your brain with the understanding that it will refuse to leave.

The word *chaos* is Greek and means "that which gapes wide open." It's a beautiful word. I see a wide-open mouth hungry to swallow the world's knowledge. I do not fear chaos; I welcome it. Chaos for me cannot be still: I make it move! I gallop as fast as I can along its path, to keep the pace of my excitement high. I must not lose the passion that drives me.

In chaos, all is possible. Every incoming idea is welcomed, with no regard for reality. Forget time, money or reason; embrace a brimming universe! Because if you start with rules, your creation will be stillborn.

But ideas should not be left floating around aimlessly; I tie them to one another—in no particular order—with the rope of intuition. They are my prisoners; I know where to find them at all times. This gives me power and freedom: I can break rules, I can be daring.

Where do those ideas come from?

I have amassed considerable archival material throughout my life: clippings, journals, specialized books, objects, iconographies on specific topics, posters, programs, random notes . . .

I keep this material in innumerable files. Some topics sleep in a single folder, others fill an entire trunk. When I am in search of ideas, I go through the files that I suspect hide gems or mysterious ingredients that may become part of my personal **parkour** and—like Jean-Baptiste Grenouille, the master perfumer in Patrick Süskind's novel *Perfume*—I extract their essence.

Can you give examples of such files?

No. In this particular case, examples would be misleading. So let's have it all!

MAGIC, STREET-JUGGLING, HIGH-WIRE WALKING, ROCK CLIMBING, BULL-FIGHTING, TEXTS, LANGUAGES, EIGHTEENTH-CENTURY BARN BUILDING, HAND TOOLS, PICKPOCKET, LOCK-PICKING, CRIME, CORDAGE, KNOTS, RIGGING, RUE LAPLACE, SAINT JOHN THE DIVINE, DRAWINGS, SACRED GEOMETRY, GYPSY, CHILDREN'S BOOKS, GRAPHICS, IMAGES, COSTUMES, MUSIC . . .

Hold on, some of this is obscure. What is "Rue Lapl—"

Wait!

. . . PHOTOGRAPHS, CHESS, THEATER, TRAVELS, GREAT RESTAURANTS, COOKING, WINES, ENGINEERING, ALTERNATIVE LIVING SYSTEMS, SURVIVAL, BRIDGES, BLACKSMITHING, FILMS, PEOPLE, LECTURES, WORKSHOPS, SCALE MODELS, QUIZZES & PUZZLES, ESCAPES, PROJECTS and NOS. (This last one is a chest filled with projects I developed that, for whatever reason, were turned down.)

I will also go to the special shelf where I keep the books that are most dear to me. I'll check for notes left in the margins and for press clippings I am in the habit of slipping under the covers.

And simultaneously . . .

I understand, but how does all of this—

Hold on!

. . . and simultaneously with this frantic hunt, I welcome the avalanche of thoughts coming my way. However tiny, however absurd, anything that passes through my mind gets caught in my net. Organization? At this stage I have no use for it!

Why an avalanche? Why not a neat, manageable stack?

Because from the start I place myself in a state of extreme focus and urgency about the subject at hand. I am frenzied, you could say.

Excess rules! Leaving something important behind would be a giant mistake. So I amass . . . until later, when the intellectual law of selection confiscates what's not essential.

Pick two topics at random from your excessive list, and use them to illustrate this process of "intellectual industry" that inhabits you.

Sure.

LOCK-PICKING and CHILDREN'S BOOKS.

These days, unless you're a certified locksmith, if you're caught with "burglar tools" in your pocket, you go directly to jail—three years. Thus, a criminal lock-picker learns to make his own tools, wherever he goes.

Lock-picking (which I learned from poorly designed clandestine manuals, CIA pamphlets and the book of trial and error) is based on a simple fact: a system involving parts designed to function in harmony with one another can do so only if the system is imperfect—that is, if there is a minuscule space between the parts. Craftsmen call this "mechanical tolerance."

Without such tolerance, a door would not open; a key would not turn in a lock; the world as we know it would not function.

The art of lock-picking consists of exploiting mechanical tolerance by introducing tiny metal tools inside a locked mechanism and rearranging its moving parts until it opens.

Why did the "hot" topic of lock-picking jump to mind? Joy! I take pleasure in finding imperfections in a system; I use them as tiny portals through which I sneak in, to explore, to understand, to create.

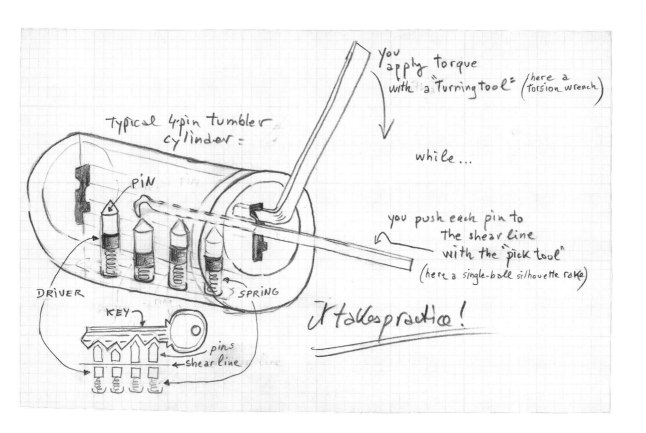

To turn to my other topic, CHILDREN'S BOOKS, it's joy again: I delight in children's books.

But mostly the ones I make.

It started when I wanted to remind my daughter, Gypsy, that her traveling father was thinking lovingly about her from far away—

I would tear striking images from magazines and mix them up with text and rough drawings I'd quickly make with thick markers. Minutes later, with the help of scissors and adhesive tape, a simple story was born and a one-of-a-kind album was assembled and put in the mail.

As I kept making them, the stories became more interesting, the drawings more sophisticated and the finished products more "professional-looking."

Soon, I was giving children's books to friends for their kids' birthdays. That's why to this day I always keep my IMAGES portfolio full.

And why do homemade children's books illustrate so well my creative process? Perhaps because it surprises me how an imposed starting point (sometimes I ask the kids to provide a character, an animal, a color, a time, for their story)—or an existing series of images (the ones I tear from magazines) opens my imagination in an instant, leading to an utterly personal, original result.

Okay. So these are elements in the avalanche, the frenzy and the excess. Now what do you do with the whole chaotic pile?

I allow it to slumber.

I let its powder sprinkle my mind, which reminds me of Simon Verity, the master stone carver who for years could be seen with stone dust in his hair, hitting his chisel with his mallet—*toc-toc, toc-toc-toc*—against the blocks of the Portal of Paradise at the Cathedral of St. John the Divine. By the end of the day his dark hair had turned handsomely gray, sprinkled with minuscule particles of limestone. The next morning, he came to work with the powder still clinging to his head, wearing it all day like a crown, smiling like a prince.

Then I take a break.

For example, thinking about this book, I'll play awhile with the concept of its cover.

Although I'm aware it is the graphic designer, not the author, who designs the cover, this fooling around is far from pointless: it adds lines to the switchboard of my ongoing creative network; it provides new mental connections that will surface—somewhere, someday, book or no book—when I wake them up. I'm fond of triggers.

After all, I'm the person who ordered a magnificent door handle from a blacksmith and upon receiving it declared: "Now that I have a way to open the door, all I need to do is build a barn around it!"

Oh! And to deal with what you call the *chaotic pile*, I now start a fresh filing container, dedicated to the project, which will stand open on my desk until completion of the work.

With separate indexed folders?

Now you're getting it!

Yes, with separate indexed folders (color coded, of course) that cover all aspects of the endeavor I am building—from excavation to opening celebration.

I'll keep old drafts in the back of the container, and in the front I'll have a large open envelope labeled À CLASSER (to file) where I'll throw things that I will sort out when I feel like it.

How long do you stay with chaos?

Until *order* emerges. Which it does, at its own pace.

And the space between chaos and order also gets my full attention. For me, it is the oft-neglected void between particles—particles of artistic nature—that changes beauty into perfection. Why are we mesmerized when we look at the stars? Because of the space between them! Can music be defined in part by the void between its notes, as the supreme wire-walk proves dependent on the ever-so-brief suspension between each of the *funambule's* steps? Yes.

Believe it or not, chaos always brings order.

I help in a deceptively simple manner.

I fish topics from the pile.

Then I file them in the open container, adding here and there a little link, a little thought.

Do you use any tools at this stage of the process?

Tools?

My fingers, my eyes, my brain.

For writing, a fountain pen with sepia ink. Adhesive tape and glue if I have the urge to cover the walls with key words, which I call *master words*.

We're miles from the laptop.

For me, the tactile experience provides a tangible link between what I formulate and the solid creation I must achieve.

Try using a pencil in the early stages of your own undertakings. Notice how your fingers absentmindedly play with the pencil while you're thinking. (Mine performs somersaults around my fingers.)

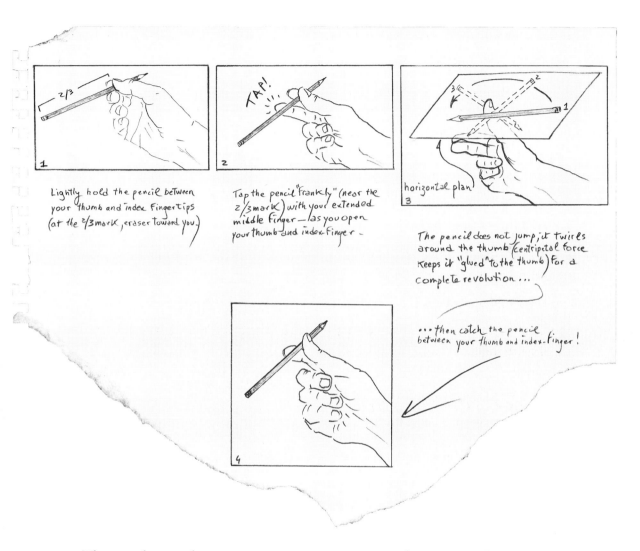

1 Lightly hold the pencil between your thumb and index fingertips (at the 2/3 mark, eraser toward you.)

2 Tap the pencil "frankly" (near the 2/3 mark) with your extended middle finger — as you open your thumb and index finger —

3 horizontal plan

The pencil does not jump, it twirls around the thumb (centripetal force keeps it "glued" to the thumb) for a complete revolution ...

... then catch the pencil between your thumb and index-finger!

The pencil moves because it is impatient to receive orders to write. Some people chew their pencils as they think—as if to extract the creative juices from their tongues to give to the writing instrument.

Consider it a blessing when your pencil needs sharpening. During that interruption your mind must hold on to a thought not yet "at hand." Look! It bounces back and forth like a child impatient to go play.

Welcome all those side motions, all these delays; they keep your imagination on the dance floor!

So you follow something of a recipe!

Hmm.

Actually, no. I think of all my steps as unpremeditated. They just happen when I set my horse loose at full gallop. Another theory of mine: turning in circles and getting lost is important! You find yourself when you get lost. And there can be no distractions. I must work nonstop.

But you have to sleep.

We spend almost a third of our lives asleep and a third of that time dreaming. The brain areas that restrict our thinking to the familiar and the logical are much less active during REM sleep; I take advantage of that.

I write and solve problems in my sleep.

How do you do that?

When I'm about to fall asleep, I place one unsolved problem, one only, under my pillow—metaphorically speaking, of course.

Once the opacity of sleep has sheltered my mind from the outside world, my subconscious decides on the right direction and travels at sonic speed. It retrieves the solution I need, which sails from outer space to paint my whirling inner space. When the motion stops, I wake up.

I must immediately jot down the solution my unconscious holds at its fingertips, or else the whole thing evaporates in the moonlight.

Yesterday I fell asleep with one precise question inside my head: *Are genius discoveries the music of chance?* I wished for an answer in a single sentence, however long.

During my sleep, fifty-five words came dancing. When the music abruptly stopped, each hurried to find a chair. Believe it or not, the chairs were in the order of a full answer to my question. I woke up and wrote it down:

Sometimes, yes: after hearing too many times Michael Corleone's long scream of despair at the end of The Godfather: Part III, *the editor working on the film temporarily muted the first half of the scream and came up with an accidental yet magisterial cinematographic effect that was kept in the final version of the movie.*

I also write effortlessly when I fly. At thirty thousand feet, the words that I could not capture during sleep float around in the rarefied, cold air and are sucked in by the vacuum the aircraft creates in its wake . . . which collects them like a magnet and brings them right to my seat.

Why do you think I always place a pad and pen under my seat belt?

You're crazy!

A compliment I appreciate.

The scent of order

The con man, the bank robber, the illegal wire-walker all begin a coup in the same way: they collect information about their target. The CIA agent preparing for an op does the same, but calls it *gathering intelligence.*

The process may involve steaming open a sealed envelope, zooming in on satellite images, or—in the case of my adventure at the World Trade Center—quick-changing into an architect's disguise in order to "borrow" a blueprint from the construction site.

Whatever it takes, in preparation for a coup I always "do my homework," an expression I despise because for me—be it under strict deadline or with the world against me—the action it describes always spells adventure, never work.

Still writing by hand, I make a complete list of what my research has produced.

But the list is always too long and some entries are not relevant to the project I'm pursuing. Impatiently, I start editing: No time! Let's go! Gloves off! Give no quarter!—as medieval axe-wielding warriors used to scream across the battlefield. The result—raw, as I like it—is not alphabetized or sorted in any other way.

This semi-organized chaos forces me to go through the entire list each time I want to find something. And the repetitive scanning unconsciously drives me to dismiss the redundant and the unworthy while validating the most important elements.

Today, working on this book, my first list is a two-page eclectic enumeration that includes some intriguing notions—TERRITORY, USELESSNESS, NEGATIVE SPACE, VULNERABILITY and IMPROVISED WEAPONS—each with thoughts and stories reverberating inside my head. For instance, if I see ARTS COLLUSION, I think about going to Thailand for a performance. I do not bring trunks filled with preconceived elements—costume, music and ideas. It would be as if the country were of no importance. Instead I bring the minimum (props

I've trained, tools I work with) and have my costume inspired by Thai style, my music influenced by Thai compositions, my ideas nourished by Thai culture, history and spirit.

If my eyes land on SIMPLICITY & ELEGANCE, I see the continually creating designer Ken Carbone. He always surprises me (he says I always surprise him).

When Ken agreed to design my barn book, the first thing he did was change its title: *A Square Peg in a Round Hole* became *A Square Peg*. With the same nod to simplicity, he transformed a thick manuscript crowded with drawings into an exquisite, almost Japanese-like album, full of white!

Clarity. Simplicity. Balance. Perfection.

Like a secret agent, I continue *processing my intelligence*. I add words where needed. I use stars or question marks to give ratings.

That's list number two.

The indubitable SPATIAL ALCHEMY, AUTODIDACT, PRIDE and PERFECTION get one star; the indecisive ARROGANCE, CHEATING and USELESS INVENTIONS merit at the moment only a question mark.

Then, to marry certain notions, I create links (*créer des liens* in French, the definition Antoine de Saint-Exupéry in *The Little Prince* gives to the verb *apprivoiser*—a term generally rendered as "to tame," but essentially untranslatable into English).

This process generates list number three, which I share with you here, more for you to glance at than to read thoroughly.

Notice how FIGHT FACILITY pairs with BODY LANGUAGE, for example, and connects to SCHEDULES, SELF-CONTROL and QUESTION THE QUESTION . . .

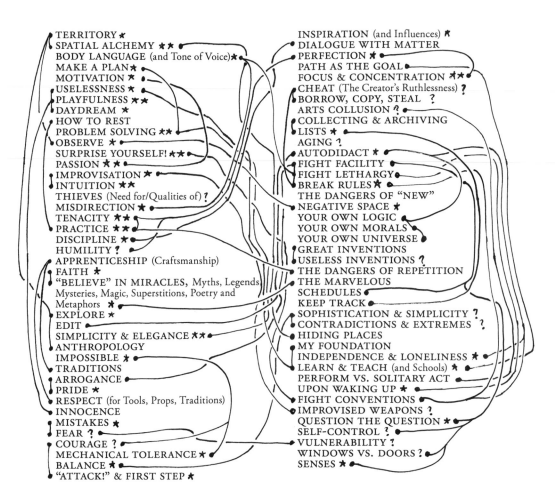

TERRITORY ★
SPATIAL ALCHEMY ★ ★
BODY LANGUAGE (and Tone of Voice) ★
MAKE A PLAN ★
MOTIVATION ★
USELESSNESS ★
PLAYFULNESS ★ ★
DAYDREAM ★
HOW TO REST
PROBLEM SOLVING ★ ★
OBSERVE ★
SURPRISE YOURSELF! ★ ★
PASSION ★ ★
IMPROVISATION ★
INTUITION ★ ★
THIEVES (Need for/Qualities of) ?
MISDIRECTION ★
TENACITY ★ ★
PRACTICE ★ ★
DISCIPLINE ★
HUMILITY ?
APPRENTICESHIP (Craftsmanship)
FAITH ★
"BELIEVE" IN MIRACLES, Myths, Legends
Mysteries, Magic, Superstitions, Poetry and
Metaphors ★
EXPLORE ★
EDIT
SIMPLICITY & ELEGANCE ★ ★
ANTHROPOLOGY
IMPOSSIBLE ★
TRADITIONS
ARROGANCE
PRIDE ★
RESPECT (for Tools, Props, Traditions)
INNOCENCE
MISTAKES ★
FEAR ?
COURAGE ?
MECHANICAL TOLERANCE ★
BALANCE ★
"ATTACK!" & FIRST STEP ★

INSPIRATION (and Influences) ★
DIALOGUE WITH MATTER
PERFECTION ★
PATH AS THE GOAL
FOCUS & CONCENTRATION ★ ★
CHEAT (The Creator's Ruthlessness) ?
BORROW, COPY, STEAL ?
ARTS COLLUSION ?
COLLECTING & ARCHIVING
LISTS ★
AGING ?
AUTODIDACT ★
FIGHT FACILITY
FIGHT LETHARGY
BREAK RULES ★
THE DANGERS OF "NEW"
NEGATIVE SPACE ★
YOUR OWN LOGIC
YOUR OWN MORALS
YOUR OWN UNIVERSE
GREAT INVENTIONS
USELESS INVENTIONS ?
THE DANGERS OF REPETITION
THE MARVELOUS
SCHEDULES
KEEP TRACK
SOPHISTICATION & SIMPLICITY ?
CONTRADICTIONS & EXTREMES ?
HIDING PLACES
MY FOUNDATION
INDEPENDENCE & LONELINESS ★
LEARN & TEACH (and Schools) ★
PERFORM VS. SOLITARY ACT
UPON WAKING UP ★
FIGHT CONVENTIONS
IMPROVISED WEAPONS ?
QUESTION THE QUESTION ★
SELF-CONTROL ?
VULNERABILITY ?
WINDOWS VS. DOORS ?
SENSES ★

Finally, I rearrange the list in accordance with the links I have established and I get rid of the connecting lines.

That's list number four, not yet final, but you may read it.

OBSERVE ✦
EXPLORE ★
ANTHROPOLOGY ★
TERRITORY ★
SPATIAL ALCHEMY ★★
NEGATIVE SPACE ★
HIDING PLACES

BODY LANGUAGE (and Tone of Voice) ★
MISDIRECTION ↗
FIGHT LETHARGY
UPON WAKING UP ★

MAKE A PLAN ✱
PROBLEM SOLVING ★★
SIMPLICITY & ELEGANCE ★★
GREAT INVENTIONS
USELESS INVENTIONS ¿

MOTIVATION ★
PASSION ★★

PRACTICE ★★
TENACITY ★★
THE DANGERS OF REPETITION
DISCIPLINE ★
HOW TO REST
FOCUS & CONCENTRATION ★★
HUMILITY ?
DIALOGUE WITH MATTER
PERFECTION ★

INTUITION ★★
IMPROVISATION ★
IMPROVISED WEAPONS ?

THIEVES (Need for/Qualities of) ?

APPRENTICESHIP (Craftsmanship)
RESPECT (for Tools, Props, Traditions)
TRADITIONS

FAITH ★
"BELIEVE" in MIRACLES (and in Myths,
Legends, Mysteries, Magic, Superstitions, Poetry,
Metaphors and the Marvelous) ★

IMPOSSIBLE ★
COURAGE ?
"ATTACK!" & FIRST STEP ★
MECHANICAL TOLERANCE ★

BALANCE ★
SOPHISTICATION & SIMPLICITY ?
CONTRADICTIONS & EXTREMES ?

MISTAKES ★
FEAR ?
VULNERABILITY ?

INSPIRATIONS (and Influences) ★

BREAK THE RULES ★
FIGHT CONVENTIONS
SURPRISE YOURSELF! ★★
CHEAT (The Creator's Ruthlessness) ?
BORROW, COPY, STEAL ?
ARROGANCE
PRIDE ★
AUTODIDACT ★
YOUR OWN LOGIC
YOUR OWN MORAL
YOUR OWN UNIVERSE
INDEPENDENCE & LONELINESS ★

ARTS COLLUSION ?
PERFORM VS. SOLITARY ACT

COLLECTING & ARCHIVING
LISTS ★
KEEP TRACK

AGING ?

FIGHT FACILITY
EDIT
SELF-CONTROL ?
QUESTION THE QUESTION ★
SCHEDULES

THE DANGERS OF "NEW"

MY FOUNDATION
LEARN & TEACH (Schools) ★
SENSES ★
USELESSNESS ★
PLAYFULNESS ★★
INNOCENCE
DAYDREAM ★
WINDOWS VS. DOORS ?
PATH AS THE GOAL

Making lists is my way of raking ideas into a critical mass before I work them out. While my pen scribbles and *order* settles in, my imagination runs ahead, anticipating creation.

I invite you to be curious about where your passion leads, to transport its explosive demeanor into the kind of chaos that finds order. What are the wonders with which you wish your creative cornucopia to be filled when you wake up in the middle of the night? List them!

((((((((((((parkour))))))))))))

Spelling the French word with a *k* does not change the essence of the thing: parkour has been around for a long time.

It started in France. People in the countryside found a way to let their creative physicality explode, for joy and good health, by running a special course made up of individual segments that mixed gymnastic achievements with playfulness—an activity that became known as *"faire un parcour."*

I remember as a little kid being brought with my sister to La Forêt de Meudon (a vast wood on the outskirts of Paris) for early-Sunday-morning parcours directed by our father. We had to walk on tree trunks across streams, crawl under bushes and climb rocks. What I liked very much were the little competitions that here and there interrupted our jogging: throwing a pebble from afar to demolish a pyramid of stones; creating the most skips across a pond; collecting in a minute the most items whose names started with a given letter of the alphabet. These little challenges seemed to happen by chance; it did not occur to me, young as I was, that they had been planted in our path. The parcours we were enjoying in 1954 came from "La Méthode Hébert," created by the influential physical educator Georges Hébert, which was growing in popularity at the time. It was a great test of agility, balance, precision and imagination.

When I was a teenager on vacation in the Jura Mountains, my favorite activity aside from bouldering was to go to the middle of a roaring brook and run toward its source by jumping from rock to rock. Stopping meant being thrown into the water by my own momentum, so I acquired a special technique that had me bouncing nonstop from one rock to another. In midair I had to make the split-second decision where to land next. I became so good at it that I was able upon each brief landing to scream the name of a letter from the Russian alphabet (a language I was teaching myself).

And then the parcour took over the city of Paris. Monuments and façades of buildings replaced rocks and trees. Of course a certain amount of illegality was involved, as you're not ordinarily permitted to climb a lamppost, balance on a train track or leap from roof to roof singing!

It became a sport, then a sport of sorts, then a novel activity that reached America and spread elsewhere throughout the world. Today, parkour, with thousands of practitioners, has turned into a way of living, almost a philosophy—with its own ethics, followers and gods.

I delight in watching a champion negotiate a short parkour with complexity, fluidity, speed, playfulness and elegance.
Surely parkour has a place in any manifesto on creativity.

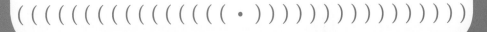

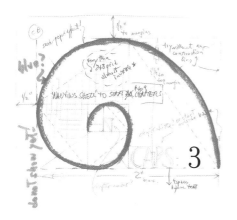

3 THE SAFE HOUSE

As I keep adding items to my filing container, it distends into a large coffer, then gives up.

It's now obvious: I need a vessel the size of Noah's Ark!

I need . . .

No one has to know, but in a remote territory not found on any map, in secrecy, my mind is assembling a mysterious lodge of imposing proportions that will shelter the most complex machinery unknown to man.

Under cover of night, I hastily empty my overstuffed coffer. But I am careful: the pile must retain its organization.

I run away and I'm back soon, dragging behind me an immense sail that I've managed to tear from an old ship in one of Turner's oil paintings (we are inside my daydream now—anything is allowed).

With this makeshift tarp, I temporarily protect the pile.

But the wind blows, the sky threatens; my intellectual mountain is in danger of being swept away!

I must secure the precious cargo at once.

Thin-air construction

Years of architectural study and engineering planning, months of daily construction, weeks of indoor finishing take place inside my head in a matter of seconds.

With the eyes of your imagination—look over there!

A large edifice now stands.

Its exterior borrows from the world history of architecture and features (hidden or in plain sight) several examples of my favorite proportion: the elusive and magnificent **Golden Mean**. Its windowless walls are indestructible. Its flat roof (accessible only by a camouflaged trapdoor) has a landing pad for my private helicopter, should I need to escape.

Each floor, column-free, is dedicated to one specific theme of my project—one "family." On every floor, each of the different-sized and -shaped rooms (giant safes, actually) will house only one subtheme—one distinguished member of that family.

Moving day

Now I fill the rooms.

As I bring material inside—more and more, faster and faster—ramps, stairs, corridors, elevators and conveyor belts show up magically to facilitate my task. What I stack in a room finds itself instantly organized on solid shelves that materialize from thin air. When I leave the room, a door suddenly appears—it already carries the label of what's inside—and locks itself behind me!

Let's be clear: I am talking about a figment of my imagination here, a non-existent structure that my mind constructs to house everything I need to pull off a creative coup. I build one each time I embark on an artistic "crime."

Finally protected, the book I am writing, the illegal wire-walk I am planning, whatever the nature of the next escapade I'm contemplating, is right here in its entirety; but in thousands of pieces.

In order to bring my creative adventure to fruition, I will visit this fortress, this safe house, many, many times. Gradually I will assemble the pieces of the jigsaw puzzle I have stored here. Finished, it will provide the ideas, moods and ingredients that will feed my dream.

Sneak-in

If I invite you to join me for a furtive visit, would you say yes?

After all, isn't a discreet scouting trip to the scene of the crime-to-be a mandatory prelude to any criminal act—a bank robbery, for example? It's called *staking the joint*.

CREATIVITY

I still remember my first illegal scouting of the nearly completed Twin Towers, after years in France planning my World Trade Center walk.*

Emerging from a long subway ride, I'm confronted with the inhuman verticality of the towers. Their size dictates that my dream is impossible. Yet I sneak onto the construction site and find my way to the top of one tower (at the time it didn't matter which one). There, again, the word *impossible* appears, this time strung between the rooftops—IM-POS-SI-BLE—but instead of making me give up, it prompts me to immediately embark on the final planning of my "crime"!

But I am not a trespasser in this imaginary place. I am the owner-builder (in the Middle Ages, my title would have been *Master of the Works*); then why the need to "sneak in"? Is it because the safe house smells of mystery, harbors treasures, is filled with secret places? Passwords are needed to travel from floor to floor. Codes must be entered to penetrate any room. A sophisticated security system has been installed at great imaginary cost. The entrance portal—a trompe-l'oeil, of course—must never be left wide-open, but kept ajar for just the fleeting time it takes a human form to glide in sideways.

Indeed, "sneak-in" is appropriate!

*"First Vision, First Visit," in my 2002 book *To Reach the Clouds* (New York: North Point Press, 2002), republished as *Man on Wire* (New York: Skyhorse, 2008).

But before we enter, let me talk to you about what our visit requires: secrecy and urgency.

A revelation concerning secrets

Inside the safe house there is an entire floor reserved for SECRETS.

Secrets are like gifts: the former a joy to reveal, the latter a pleasure to offer. Secrets are vital. They connect us to our childhood, to the hide-and-seek-playing youth within us.

The first thing I did when I entered the broom-closet I call Rue Laplace* (which I was to occupy illegally for forty-five years—it was too small to be considered a legal living space) was to scratch with the tine of a fork at the grout around a floor tile until I was able to lift the tile free. Below, I dug a mini-dungeon the size of my fist—a place to deposit golden coins I never got. Then I replastered around the opening to restore the floor so perfectly that I could not lift the tile even using my fingernails—I had to employ the suction of a toilet plunger.

Throughout my years of living in Rue Laplace, with help from magnets and springs, I continued to rig the space with more hiding places.

When I first met Professor Rudolf Omankowsky, Sr.—Papa Rudy, the extraordinary old circus veteran and wire-walker from Czechoslovakia who would become my mentor—I asked for technical advice and rigging lessons. He agreed . . . on condition that I buy each of the "high-wire secrets" he imparted. I would purchase a knot, a way to connect the cable

---

*Situated at 10 Rue Laplace, in the fifth arrondissement of Paris.

to an anchor, the knowledge of which type of wire-rope was needed for a given job.

The sale of those secrets went on for several months, until our flourishing friendship rendered such transactions obsolete. (Believe me, having to pay did not add to the aura of enlightenment!)

Wait! More on secrets.

I once read a voluminous study on one of my favorite subjects: survival.

I learned that besides all the obvious qualities that help one to survive in catastrophic situations, two unlikely traits are essential: a sense of humor and—if you are in a group—the ability to keep to yourself, meaning not to reveal much about who you are, to hold on to your privacy. Which I translate as "to remain secretive."

This makes sense to me. If you must draw on all your strength and talents in order to cheat death—in order to do the *im-pos-si-ble*, do not give yourself away, do not spread yourself thin, because if you dilute yourself, you'll wash away—*Pfft!* Like that . . . you'll be gone.

It is essential for the chemistry of my creative process that I visit my invisible safe house secretly, as if it were forbidden. Each time I enter, I must be in a state of trespassing; I must feel at risk, an inch away from being caught. And of course I must avoid being captured at all cost!

A taste of urgency

When I reach a room to retrieve something, I must enter as fast as I can, remain inside for the briefest of time, all the while feeling like a spy with a deadly deadline.

When I'm busy creating, I hear every second ticking, I taste the urgency. I worry. What if my imagined world abruptly surrenders to blunt reality? What if the hazards of inactivity kidnap me?

Every morning he ran to his cable, leaping over the grass so the dew would not weigh him down . . . That's how I introduced my daily aerial rehearsals, in the treatise I wrote at eighteen, dedicated to my self-apprenticeship in the art of wire-walking.*

Why run? Why not walk?

Impatience—to me, a great virtue—is a branch of the Tree of Passion.

"Life is short" was the tune I started humming at . . . hmm . . . twelve years old! My daily activities suffer each and every day. Why? Because between sunrise and sunset there are not enough hours.

Observe animals in the wild. They eat fast, as if their lives depend on it. Well, they do. When the impala grazes in the savanna, its head buried in high grass, it cannot see the crawling predator approaching. The leopard often drags its lunch at great expense of energy onto the highest branch of a tree. Eat and keep watch. Or be eaten.

When facing a bunch of delicious grapes, to this day I still behave like the kid I was: I pick one grape with my left fingers, bring it to my mouth in one swift move, chew and swallow, while my right fingers have already begun the exact same movement. I repeat the symmetrical back-and-forth motion like a well-oiled machine until all the grapes are gone. Is this the remnant of some prehistoric survival instinct—"What I swallow rapidly

*Philippe Petit, *On the High Wire*, trans. Paul Auster (New York: Random House, 1985).

won't be stolen by my neighbor"—or simply the playful behavior of a voracious child?

I've seen Time devour Art with avidity—and I love it!

Ephemeral art never fails to inspire me, rekindles my creative energy when it has reached the amber state.

I watched a young man armed with only a wet broom trace the simplest of calligraphy—the word *freedom*—on a pale gray asphalt sidewalk. Each letter was born black as ink; but within minutes, each found its death, gray on gray, as the warm asphalt evaporated the message.

When I talk to someone about a project dear to me, the speed of my delivery is the ambassador of my excitement. Oh, how rewarding when such contagious behavior induces my interlocutor to reply in similar machine-gun fashion!

Impatience. Excitement. The fight against time. Ebullience.

All of these probably explain why I became, with lots of practice, a master at interrupting—not such a great virtue, I've been told.

Virtual visit

Secretly, quickly, unlock the heavy portal and hold it open just a bit so I can squeeze through. You follow, as my shadow. Perfect, we're in.

Now lock the door.

Just as I tell friends I invite along for a crossing on my practice wire seven feet off the ground, I say to you: "Please stay right behind me. Hold on to my shoulders. Place your feet exactly where I've stepped. Do not speak, only whisper."

In that same way, we negotiate the long, dark, inclined corridor in front of us (which, you might have noticed, I borrowed from the Great Pyramid of Cheops). In a moment your eyes will adapt to the semi-obscurity . . .

. . . in a flash, an eternity stretches . . .

. . . and just as quickly, we are retracing our steps down the long, dark corridor and standing once again by the portal! You're thinking, *The mission has been aborted: our labyrinthine visit is over.* But that's not what happened.

Let me assure you, we've been here for three days and three nights. We've entered every room. You've seen everything.

Yes, inside this place, as inside a thought, objects change their molecular arrangement, geography loses its bearing, reason abandons reason, time distorts.

Now, please do tell: what were your favorite sights?

Was it the first room we entered, the *Organization Room*—with its hundreds of exercise-books (some three inches thick) that document my preparations for major high-wire walks, divided into sections such as *Site Study, History and Geology, Weather Forecast, Rigging Solutions, Crew, Equipment Inventory, Performance Ideas, Show Description and Timing, Costume, Music*?

I saw you open a notebook at random. You were intrigued by a little brush of natural fiber glued to a page—fibers from the yucca cactus that the ancestors of the indigenous people whose land I was going to walk over used to twist into sacred cords. I intended to wear one as a ceremonial belt for my walk: as homage and to ensure a safe journey.

And the globe? You liked the globe—in the *Travel Room*, with the pair of purple slippers at the door? You put them on and were instantly retracing all the walking journeys of my life, all over the globe. And when you paused (upside down), the pages of my travel sketchbooks flipped by, revealing all the curious things I had stopped to draw.

What about the *Body Language Room*? Its collection of thousands of photographs of human gestures from all parts of the world might help me choreograph a prolonged entrance onto an oversized stage . . . or deal with a crowd pressing in on me too tightly during an outdoor improvised magic show . . . or assemble a comic scene for street-juggling . . . or hone the slow-motion arrival of an aerial crossing that includes a greeting by city officials . . .

Did you appreciate the display, images multiplied to infinity by mirrored walls?

On the triforium floor under the flying buttresses, did you hear the whispers and giggles coming from the tiny *Storytelling Vault*, filled with anecdotes and episodes—all of them true—that I will choose from to illustrate this book?

Now, please, close your eyes and look at the sky! I mean: put your head back and close your eyes, and let me sprinkle you with a bit of *I'm no longer able to remember* stardust . . .

Then, very gently, step out of my imagined world and return to reality.

Open your eyes.

You're back! And I can safely ask if you have any memory of our visit, because your answer will be: "What visit?"

But what are those purple slippers doing on your feet?

Never mind . . .

Exit

Fresh air welcomes us.

Before we close the heavy portal, on the inside I glue a precious document: my *Table of Contents* of the day, where each consecutive phase of the coup I am hatching is clearly detailed.

Outside, the pile is gone.

The giant sail flew back to its ship. Day and night (but mostly night—you know by now my predilection for covert operations), I'll sneak back in, to keep serving whatever project has me struggling.

Now I urge you to begin building your own safe house at the moment you begin building your dream.

A hidden fissure through which the initiated can pass in order to travel through Time, your imaginary fortress will become—and will remain— an essential portal to your creativity.

We vanish into the foggy dawn, after one long, last glance toward the invisible formidable fortress that I now call my *Cathedral of Creativity*, my *Palace of Knowledge*, without which no book, no walk, no creative crime of mine would ever, could ever, happen—and that's one of my many secrets.

(((((((((((**Golden Mean**)))))))))))

No painter, no architect, no composer, no choreographer, no set designer, no movie director, no equestrian, no thief should pursue his or her vocation in ignorance of the Golden Ratio.

1.618033988749894820 . . .

This is *phi* (Φ).

Wait, wait!

The Golden Ratio, also known as the Golden Mean and the Golden Section, was christened "Divina Proportione" by the Italian monk Luca Pacioli di Borgo, who in 1509 in Venice published a splendid treatise on the subject, illustrated by a friend . . . Leonardo da Vinci.

Some 4,600 years ago, the Egyptians based the dimensions of the Great Pyramid of Giza on the Golden Ratio. The Greek sculptor Phidias (ca. 490–430 BC) made extensive use of it in his work; the concept of *phi* was named after him. The Parthenon, which contained sculpture by him, was laid out on a Golden Rectangle, and its design contains many instances of it. Circa 300 BC, the Greek mathematician Euclid, author of the oldest existing geometry treatise, writes about "dividing a segment in mean and extreme reason" and defined what would later be referred to as the Golden Number. In Rome in the first century BC, Vitruvius applied the Golden Mean to architecture and developed in his ten-volume *De Architectura* the notion of arithmetic harmony with "the perfect symphony of the proportions" found in the human body. Fibonacci (ca. 1175–1240), the Italian mathematician celebrated for having introduced to Europe the use of Arabic digits, studied a suite of numbers whose correlation tends toward the Golden Number, 1.618 . . .

Let's add Shakespeare, Mozart and Le Corbusier at the other end of a long list of enthusiastic practitioners . . .

What is *phi*? What is the Golden Mean?

A harmony of proportions created by nature, which immensely pleases the eye and soul of humans.

The Golden Ratio governs the growth of the *Nautilus pompilius* shell (which I chose as the emblem that opens each chapter of this book). The distribution of seeds in the cactus plant, sunflower, pinecone and pineapple illustrates the Fibonacci Sequence and conforms exactly to the Golden Spiral (a spiral that grows in accordance with the Golden Ratio).

Of course man could not resist picking up on nature's perfection. The proportion was put into words: "The Golden Mean is a length divided in such a way that the ratio of the longer part to the whole is the same as the ratio of the shorter part to the longer part." And into a formula: "The Golden Mean is the mathematical proportion obtained if a point P divides a straight line AB in such manner that AP:PB = AB:AP (a ratio expressed by *phi*, which rounds to 1.618)."

Thousands of pages have been printed on *phi*; and now, of course, there is a website, goldennumber.net!

To spy on visitors outside, to invite more brightness inside, I decide to cut a small window in the main door of the barn I have been building.

As homage to ancient discoverers, it must have the shape of a Golden Rectangle—a rectangle whose sides are related by *phi*. The Golden Rectangle is said to be the most visually satisfying of all the geometric forms. It has calming virtues, I might add.

I feel the excitement of an early mathematician-engineer as I gather pen, square and compass. I start by drawing a square ABCD, the length of each side corresponding to the window's height. I add the point M in the middle of the side AB, to create the diagonal MC, which I use as a radius to bring the arc of a circle to intersect the prolongation of the line AMB at E. Then, by drawing a vertical line from E to meet the horizontal extension of DC in F, I complete the rectangle AEFD. I experiment reducing and enlarging the rectangle simply by relocating the point D anywhere on the diagonal ED or its extension, until I finalize the size of the window.

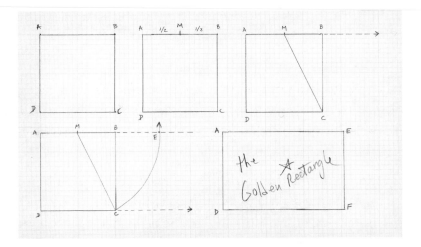

My wish has been granted: this book, once opened flat, is, like my window, a pristine Golden Rectangle.

Algebraically, mathematically, aesthetically, logically—and, fortunately, naturally—the Divine Proportion expresses a movement that keeps spiraling into infinity. We humans are merely trying to follow, but our eyes are filled with wonder.

((((((((((((((((((•))))))))))))))))))

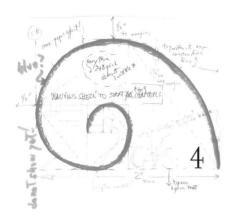

4 | SUBVERSIVE ELEMENTS

My creative process so far can be construed as simple: I invent a target from a blank canvas; I gather elements and set the crime in motion by pulling order out of chaos; I become the architect of an imaginary fortress that I visit regularly.

Now I need to shift from the *Palace of Knowledge* to the physical world, so that other elements can come into play: the way I navigate my territory, the need for tools, my negotiations with Time and other foes, and the extraordinary balance required to glue it all together.

Come along and witness how I deal with these elements—these subversive elements. Let's begin with the way I secure my creative territory, for there is a special alchemy here to be aware of and to cherish—I call it: "my spatial alchemy."

My spatial alchemy

In the journal I kept during my barn-building experience, I find the following entry:

A plastic bag dancing in the breeze might steal a second of inattention from a carpenter holding a razor-sharp framing chisel; the result might be a cut in the wrong place or even the loss of human flesh. Tripping on a piece of wood left on the ground after sawing might have the same unfortunate effect.

When I set out to build something, before I even scribe lines on a timber stock, I choose a work area where the ground is flat and clear of debris. I ensure that my sawhorses are steady and level, both lengthwise and width-wise. And I make sure that the backdrop I face (a wall, a fence, a screen of shrubs) is parallel to the posts and beams I'm working with.

In the same manner, when I scan the scene of a creative crime-to-be, when I *stake the joint*, I look for flaws or obstacles that might create disturbance or distraction. I find it crucial to "situate myself," that is, to imagine my body placement during the main phases of the coup.

Buried in the notes of my daily juggling sessions I find the following:

When I give a workshop at a circus school, I am appalled to notice how, sometimes, apprentice jugglers stand "sideways to a wall" as they practice; or face an open doorway with fellow students coming and going.

Anyone who knows how to juggle understands that the flying path of the objects thrown in the air must be kept within a vertical plane. If the juggler keeps this "panel of action" parallel to a facing wall, the objects will have a tendency to remain inside the vertical plane, the hands will "fly" the balls with more control of direction; and the juggler will not have to extend his arms or move backward to keep up with the objects; and this will keep the juggler from dropping them! (I usually don't teach this subtle spatial maneuver; I guide the student to discover it through experience.)

I am shocked to realize how few magicians are aware of what I would call "the terrain of cards."

In one of my earliest *cahiers* on prestidigitation, started nearly sixty years ago in the throes of my passion for magic, I come upon this:

> When the illusionist places a card in front of a spectator, the location of the card on the close-up mat is of major importance—it tells!
>
> If the card is close to the spectator, it is the magician's statement of confidence. It implies: "The card is so close to you that you could touch it, even turn it over, but that won't bother me!"
>
> If the card is placed far away from the spectator, it indicates mistrust: "If you move that card, the trick will fail!"

The skilled pickpocket, in a similar way, knows how a specific site communicates a specific feeling. The alcove where a bank hides its cash machine is not the place to approach a "client," who already might feel insecure there, lonely or even cornered. Instead, the master thief decides to strike in the middle of a wide, busy sidewalk, where one feels the freedom awarded by open spaces as well as the protection granted by anonymous crowds.

And no one understands the artist-to-space relation better than the bull-fighter, whose life depends on it.

At the age of seventeen, attracted by the ballet of capes but not by *the moment of truth*—the death of the animal—I joined a group of young boys in the south of France who dreamed of becoming toreros. My initiation into **the secrets of bullfighting** taught me about the "winds of territory"—a concept which imprints each of my arts.

Fanatical as I am on the subject, my attention to spatial alchemy does not carry an ounce of austerity nor does it lean toward sterility. If I'm insistent on having rules for space, my insistence includes the need to break the rules and welcome any kind of territory to entertain me, to bring me joy and surprise, to seduce me . . . with unexpected curves! No rigidity, please.

And curves can be practical.

I once heard a guide leading a visit to Nottingham Castle explain that the high tunnels and covered passages surrounding the main building had been laid out on a curvaceous route because, in the era of knights, when riding a horse was a common part of everyday life, the architects knew how to prevent horses from being scared (and blinded) by a patch of bright light waiting at the end of a straight tunnel.

But most of all, curves are pleasing to me. My last travel sketchbook includes a sketch of a rather small garden gracing a Relais & Château in Brittany. At the top of the page, my question: *What is the secret of the charm of the garden of Le Domaine de Rochevilaine at Billiers in Morbihan?*

The answer can be found in the sketches themselves:

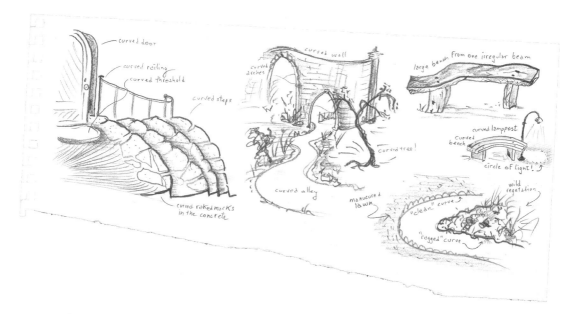

Curves.

Not a single element of the setting is straight.

The tiled steps from the hotel portal to the garden floor are arranged in a semicircle. The alleys snake gently through the grounds, and even their borders do not match—here, on one side, an even, soft curve; on the other, a series of zigzags. (Zigzagging is definitely more conducive to creativity than straight-lining, unless you're a tightrope walker! Enjoy zigging as the world zags.) All the shrubs are tortuous, not one tree has a rectilinear trunk. Even the irregular wooden benches show how the designers made use of crooked local timber.

I never feel more at home than when I step inside one of those old English cottages built in cruck-frame style—that is, whose timber frames are composed of pairs of large, naturally curved timbers that are joined at the top to support a ridge beam. Is it because man has altered nature very little, allowing the curves we see in trees outside to continue, as a roof, to shelter us, to protect us from the elements; to hold us close to the forest of our past; to transform us into poets?

All of which is to say I cannot emphasize enough the influence your surroundings have on your creativity. Think of your "theater of action" as the costume of a character in the Commedia dell'Arte! Your outfit, your mask, is as important in defining your personage as your body language. So encompass the stage and control its space.

Negative space

"What is negative space?"

A child asked me that after he heard me say that it was not so much the Twin Towers that attracted me to walk between them but the virgin *negative space* they protected between them.

I answered by drawing a quick little sketch of the kid's face, then folding the sheet in half and tracing an identical profile opposite the first. I connected the two silhouettes at the top and bottom to form a vase. "The vase is the object," I showed him, "and your face on both sides is the negative space."

I invite you to fall into the habit of noticing the negative space around you, as I do. It will open an entirely new world, it will double your perception, it will stretch your imagination, it will invite you to explore mysterious desert islands of wonders, it will make you soar, as in a dream. Better than in a dream.

If, like me, you work on the awareness of the space you inhabit, especially the negative space, you will easily be able to imagine what's not yet there, what there is for you to bring.

Start honing your sense of space (as well as your body, your tools, your props inside the space) *before* you start working.

Look around you for inspiring examples of acquired and controlled territories that offer a backyard, a meadow, a stadium for your spreading creativity!

For example, before a juggling performance on stage, I carefully imagine where one of the balls might roll and get lost if I accidentally drop it. And I create obstacles to ensure that does not happen! (When performing in the street, I'm known to cover sewer holes around my circle of chalk to prevent the balls from getting lost forever!)

You see? By doing that I'm actually foreseeing the action, the "crime," before it happens.

You're a sculptor? In your sleep, dream in three dimensions . . .

You're a writer? Visualize the chapter ahead before you set fingertips to keys!

You're a stonecutter? Mentally, chip the ashlar you're squaring before you bring the chisel's cutting edge to the limestone grain . . .

Look at this: negative space . . . upside down!

In 1971, returning to my Parisian home at midnight along the Rue du Chat Qui Pêche (the Street of the Fishing Cat, the narrowest in the city), I noticed the piece of dark sky imprisoned by the façades on both sides of the alley. I recognized the exact silhouette of the steeple of the Cathedral of Notre Dame, which I was very soon to attack with an illegal high-wire walk.

Tools

From the very beginning of my apprenticeship in my arts, my first concern (in preparation and in performance) has been the tools on which the art depends.

Tools are a natural extension of my concept of space. They are the means through which my creations take form. As such, they deserve my utmost attention—imaginative as well as practical attention.

They are often very simple and very old.

A pencil to write or draw. A rigging knife to cut a rope. A deck of cards to execute a magic trick. A framing square to lay out timber.

Tools are the extension of the craftsman's, the artist's limbs and soul. The ballet dancer must find and "form" a pair of ballet slippers (a long and painful process); the juggler must find and "teach" a top hat the right moves.

With painstaking effort, and with humility, the artist must learn to use and maintain his or her tools. My aim is to reach a harmonious dialogue with my tools. Through repetitive use I gain effortless mastery of them, and with mastery comes the respect without which, I believe, no expert craftsmanship can ever be reached.

Before a concert begins, the first violin (the concertmaster) stands up. This is the signal for the oboe—the most distinctive voice in the orchestra—to give the A pitch to the first violin, who gives it in turn to each section of the symphony orchestra.

Just so, long before your coup—your time of action—I urge you to articulate your preparations in the most practical ways.

First and foremost that means acquire the proper tools!

This is usually the easiest part of the process. The equipment needed for an illegal crossing—a hoist powerful enough to tension the wire, the thousand feet of special rope to guy-line the walk, the many custom-made contraptions needed to serve the system quickly, silently, efficiently—is no more difficult to obtain than the tools for a legally sanctioned walk.

But they have to be the "right tools for the task." They have to bring to the project the right spirit as well as the right physical behavior. My coups need both equally.

Line up your tools!

In the years that I was building my little barn, I would start each workday by lining up my tools—the hand tools of the eighteenth-century timber framer—on the workbench. I'd lay them parallel, in the order of their most frequent use, and position the razor-sharp blades away from me.

When I commence a high-wire rigging operation, I do the same. I consider the order in which the parts must be assembled. Then I lay each clamp, bolt, washer, nut, thimble, shackle and shackle pin—my tools of the day—methodically and precisely, just as a surgeon would organize his instruments before an operation.

Here is a less mechanical example, far from the grease of nuts and bolts.

Before I started my last children's book, which I decided would exhibit a debauchery of colors, I spread over my workbench all the markers, highlighting pens and colored pencils I own—all hundred and twenty of them!—along with a fine collection of Derwent graphite pencils. They all lay happily side by side, like schoolchildren awaiting the recess bell. As I admired the display, I knew something was missing. I found it in the discard pile in the corner of the atelier: a long, grooved tray, perfect for housing one category of pencils: those of perfectly cylindrical shape, which want to roll away from my fingers!

Props

When tools serve an artist performing, they change their name to "props"—a term I find unappealing in English as well as in French (*les accessoires*). Nonetheless, long ago I fell in love with my props. I protect and cherish them because they've become part of me and my arts.

When I started out, most props could not be bought from a store, the way they can be today. And those that were for sale I learned the hard way to buy at my own risk.

As I was learning magic, juggling was repeatedly mentioned as a way to improve dexterity and coordination. I had long admired how fast and fluidly jugglers could make objects fly. So at fourteen I decided to become a juggler!

I befriended a kid in a juggling troupe, and he agreed to sell me three graceful-looking clubs. Before long, I got pretty fast with my new clubs, but for some reason I wasn't fluid at all. They seemed to be flying away from me at each throw; I was constantly trying to bring them back to me.

One day, I happened to be practicing in the presence of my friend Francis Brunn, the greatest juggler in the world. He frowned, then asked: "Can I see those?"

I proudly showed him my clubs.

"Philippe!" he said. "You've been had! These are rejects, completely out of alignment, they're impossible to juggle!"

That was how I discovered I had no choice but to learn how to make my own props. It was hard work (it took me fourteen hours to make my first club), but I gained an intimacy and a sense of possession that proved essential in my dialogue with the object, and that no piece of equipment I could purchase would ever provide.

That process only deepened my understanding of how to maintain my artistic tools, how to address them—and, yes, how to talk to them.

I am often appalled to witness the sorry state of props in the rehearsal hall of circus schools I visit. Instruments are thrown around after use or piled up in a communal basket for anyone to choose from; and when they are too damaged to use, they end up in the nearest garbage can!

Most performers I knew when I was young would never show or lend (and certainly not sell or discard) the precious props they'd made for themselves, or, in rare cases, had ordered at great expense from a specialized craftsman.

Francis Brunn always covered his open trunk of props with a thick old bath towel before it left his dressing room for the backstage, prior to a performance. Supposedly, it was to protect the fragile objects, but it was a sure way to prevent someone from looking at them too closely or touching them.

I do not share my props either.

And when they die, I would never think of discarding them. I put them to rest inside a coffer, not a coffin. Sometimes I exhume them briefly to take their measurements if I'm about to make new ones, or simply to stare at them—which brings me inspiration.

When you treat your props with love and respect, they retain the life you've infused them with. Francis once gave me one of the large balls he could bounce on his forehead with devilish control, remarking: "Don't ever forget who trained her!"

Calendars and hieroglyphs

The period of time it takes me to write this book is mapped out on the giant calendar that hangs above my writing study. I see the overall schedule and I duly cross out each day as I progress.

The open squares of the week to come are rife with little invented pictograms that Kathy calls "PP's hieroglyphs."

My companion of twenty-six years reminds me that the little symbols with which I surround myself in daily life attest to the visual acuity that is a significant part of my process of creativity.

"I know," I say. "In Chapter 6, I colloquy on OBSERVATION."

The little icons scattered across the days ahead tell me what I have to do.

MONDAY:

(Back to my full three-hour practice of the three balls and the wire interrupted by a cold.)

TUESDAY: *(I have a parcel to mail.)*

WEDNESDAY: *(The car needs a checkup.)*

THURSDAY: *(Dentist appointment.)*

FRIDAY: *(Time to pick up my new glasses.)*

SATURDAY: *(My brother Alain's birthday.)*

Oh, and three days ago, scribbled indelibly in red ink on the ivory page of my diary are two tiny lightning bolts:

*(They signify a terrible argument
I had with a friend.)*

If you seek a "Festival of Hieroglyphs," then open my *cahiers* for any of my grand projects!

To me, the reappearance of visual symbols on the calendar is reminiscent of my not-too-distant return to the tangibility of terrestrial tasks after the long flight of this book; and with that will come—with a sigh of relief—the abandonment of the necessary evil tool, my MacBook Air.

Time conspiracy

A plan dedicated to the notion of time becomes a schedule—an invaluable tool that guides my long (or short) approach to any project. I rely on a schedule for my daily life as well. Since there is not enough time in the day for me to write; practice magic, juggling and the wire; draw; build; research; repair; work on languages; develop lectures; prepare workshops; and make proposals for future performances, I devise a daily program that alternates activities. I tailor it to the seasons (in winter I can rarely walk on the wire outdoors) and I rearrange it according to priorities, although Murphy ensures I can never follow my schedules scrupulously. But without them, I would be drifting hopelessly and my energy would scatter and shatter.

When it comes to an illegal walk, I decide early, even if it is too soon to decide, the ideal date for the coup. I mark it boldly on a giant calendar-of-the-year. Week after week, month after month, my eyes cannot avoid looking at the calendar. I do not mind changing the D-Day several times, under the pressure of outside circumstances . . . until the thought of postponing once again becomes unbearable or signifies to me that the project has reached its point of asphyxiation. (During my WTC adventure, the coup was postponed seventeen times before I forced myself to fix an "unmovable-whatever-the-excuse-final-final" date.)

The schedule that governs the unfolding of a coup is nothing but a detailed battle plan. It deals with the duration of a series of actions (estimated by sheer science or by guesswork—my estimations are always wrong). Such a schedule usually proves, after the fact, just good enough to make a paper airplane!

The important thing is that what I must do stays in front of me above my desk—nags at me—until I finish. For example, the calendar for this book—two feet by three—showed me how many days I gave myself to draft each chapter.

During the arduous six-and-a-half-year approach to my WTC walk, my friend, my confidant, my *fiend* was a four-by-eight-foot panel divided into little squares, an entire wall turned calendar!

In any project, as if I were a child before Christmas, I dutifully cross out a square a day to monitor my progress or to make sure I make up for being late.

A schedule also reminds me: time is of the essence, in life as well as in a project.

A schedule can feel like self-imposed jail cells—but it's also the opposite: whenever I plant in my creative path a time-bomb, a reminder, a deadline, it frees me from Time. By reminding me that I can distort Time.

The deadline feeds my impatience. And often because of that I find myself ahead!

Accomplices

"Solo integral" is the term French climbers use to refer (often with awe, at times with disdain) to climbers who negotiate a high rock face alone, without rope or artificial aid. They place their lives in the trust of their own technique, strength and spirit. For me, this is the only way to climb (I would add, "Do it barefoot or naked!")—just as walking the wire without any safety device or instruments is the only way to be a true wire-walker.

Yet an artistic crime performed solo—truly the perfect crime—is extremely rare. Almost any significant creative endeavor (should I say "regrettably"?) calls for accomplices. All my illegal wire-walks require inside men, lookouts, people to carry equipment and to follow my rigging orders. Another example would be the collaboration involved in staging a new musical, or producing a feature film—directors, writers, actors and set designers have to work together. And what about the architects, structural engineers and technical consultants who were involved in the reinforcement of a floor of New York City's Museum of Modern Art to accommodate the installation of Richard Serra's hundreds of tons of curved steel walls?

You will need—forgive me, but I'm speaking to you as a co-conspirator—to learn to acquire these "human tools," and to bend them to your project's purpose. My experience? They are the most difficult tools to find and use!

So try to choose your collaborators as carefully as you can; place character above experience, and trust your instinct more than whatever display they put on in order to be chosen. When you look into their eyes, a glint of humanity, a sparkle of passion, is far more telling than any coaxing speech they might utter, or an impressive résumé.

No matter how you choose, sooner or later you will be betrayed. Accept that.

One will give out your secret.

One will make promises and break them.

One will arrive late or give up in the midst of the project.

Or worse yet—as I can attest—one will forget to remember that taking part in the coup was the best moment of his life.

Can tools betray humans? I don't think so. You can always check on them. But humans . . . wow!

Watch bank-heist movies: each time a coup fails, it is due to human error, human limitation, human betrayal.

So trust your new accomplices, treat them with respect, communicate to them with passion, but at the same time be ruthless! Do not exercise democracy, do not think of them—or yourself. Serve only the coup; support only the dream!

I'd be remiss if I didn't talk about the most important tool of all: the human body.

A natural and wondrous extension of tools and props—actually, the ultimate tool—the body is ready to serve our art. Any art.

Take the lecturer, for example: she needs only a tongue, right? Wrong! The subtle, mostly imperceptible dance the speaker does at the pulpit, her body language, is what lends her words their foundation—is what will interest, even rivet, the audience.

The body requires, like any tool, care and maintenance as well as repair. But there is no one way to do this: everyone must decide for themselves how to keep their tools in service.

My own attitude, articulated in my treatise *On the High Wire*, is "You have to pull your body by the sleeve. Make it follow your orders. Impose!"

I care strongly, however, about fighting the body's negative inclinations.

Beware of lethargy.

Lethargy

Lethargy lurks! With its ugly green poisonous tongue sticking out, it lies in wait for the body.

I fight lethargy.

Why?

Because it reminds me of the unbecoming mien of my human condition: wanting to let go when I should keep holding on. Because it assails me in an underhanded way, by crippling my body one limb at a time (or my senses, one atom after the other) the moment I let my guard down. But mainly because lethargy destroys creativity.

And it does so, not hidden in a dark alley but in the center of town, in full daylight, right in front of everyone!

Open a modern fashion magazine, see how young models are directed by the photographer to sit or stand as if their boneless bodies contained only thin air. Their overpainted faces with pouted lips express boredom, or worse, no mood at all. They slouch, they slump, they are listless, they lean, they limp, they have no balance! As you look at them, their human decomposition becomes contagious. They put you to sleep while they elevate physical laziness (which heightens intellectual apathy) to a state of virtue.

Watching a disillusioned teenager dragging his feet has the same effect.

How do I fight lethargy?

By sharpening my senses—and loading my sleeves with a few tricks.

A few years ago, I directed *A Theater of Balance*, a master class with a select group of students at SLAM (Elizabeth Streb's Lab for Action Mechanics). How did I select the participants? By asking their preferences in movies, books and music, where they had traveled, the languages they spoke, their favorite dancers and poets . . .

But I digress!

Where was I?

Ah, yes . . .

I began the class by saying: "There are no rules here!" But then, noticing the behavior of one tired soul, I realized I actually had a rule—and added: "I do not tolerate leaning. Please do not lean on the walls or against the equipment. Oh, and I happen to have another rule: No yawning! Actually . . . now that I think of it, there are three rules. The third one is: No yawning while leaning!" These became what I now refer to as *The Streb Commandments*, but they will also work like a charm for anyone doing battle with lethargy. They work on the principle that eliminating the symptom eliminates the disease.

"Shoulders back, heels down!" my horseback-riding instructor admonished. I avoided his reprimand because I always sat well in the saddle, my back perfectly straight. But at breakfast I mentally serve myself the reminder "Sit up straight!" along with my fried eggs. The physical attitude causes me to start the day with a positive frame of mind.

If you control your posture, you will introduce more balance into your life. This simple equation should be experienced rather than learned: when you walk, when you stand, you will feel the equilibrium, which will translate into joie de vivre, which will lead you to accomplishments!

Start each day with a little dose of this exquisite self-control I call balance.

Where is balance?

Balance—one of my secrets to confront and survive the impossible!

But who can answer this: Where is balance?

I can.

Balance is everywhere. It must be everywhere for the human machine to function both physically and mentally.

But balance is prompt to dissolve.

For me, a deadly balance-disruption always creeps in immediately after a demanding high-wire walk. My energy abandons me; my faith dissipates, drained of natural stimulant; my body refuses to follow any new orders—I am suddenly bereft of balance.

To prolong the life of the dream-that-has-become-reality—and to prepare myself for the next project—I eliminate the disruption by forcefully reconstructing my balance.

Why did we forget it is balance that allowed us to rise from all fours and become bipeds? Balance in our lungs and heart allows us to breathe. The list of what balance allows is endless.

Did your parents teach you to walk across the room balancing a book on your head to acquire good posture?

In many countries, kids learn at an early age to carry water from a distant well to their village by balancing a heavy jar on their heads. (The same kids have already learned that walking five kilometers to school is a small price for education.) As I travel, I marvel at the people who walk barefoot along busy roads, calmly carrying voluminous bundles on their heads—and often heavy parcels in their hands as well. They glide effortlessly, elegantly, their stride has rhythm.

Balance has helped them find their center of gravity, has made them aware of the automatic action-reaction system our body uses. When they unload their merchandise and turn, unburdened, to talk to someone, they hold their heads up, their bodies erect, they smile a mix of health and joie de vivre.

The rest of us, sitting most of the time bent over our computers or at the wheel of a car, intent upon driving as fast and as close as possible to our destination—no longer traveling on foot, rarely walking barefoot, not balancing anything on our heads—are, in fact, missing many of the wonders our human body is capable of.

Lean on balance

To the students attending my master class on balance I introduce early on the principle of *how to hold on to something.*

As each student attempts to walk a wire without a balancing-pole, seven feet off the floor, I offer to one of their moving hands the support of a genuine Irish shillelagh, handmade from blackthorn, which I hold above my head; but I make sure to move the stick up and down, following the movement of the student's hand.

Moving is key: my aim is to contribute in an unhindered manner to the stability of the walker. A fixed, solid support would put the student's sense of balance to sleep.

And when the students leave class, I add to my good-byes a reminder: "A twig, not a branch!" I explain that as they continue to practice walking—say, on a rope between two trees—it's okay for them to secure their balance before taking the first step by holding on to a part of the tree for a second. But they must choose a supple twig, not a solid branch. The twig invites equilibrium; the branch wards it off.

The same applies to working out with weights in a gym. If you lift weights that are guided by rails, you are relying on the apparatus to provide balance to the lift. But if you use free weights, you remain the sole *Director of Balance*, you apply your true strength to the act through what I call "living balance."

Imagine that you return home to find a large fallen branch blocking your driveway. Are there aluminum railings on which to slide the obstacle out of the way? No? Then lift the damn thing! You can't? Aha! It's the fault of the weight machine with captive weights!

Are you left-footed?

Acquiring balance (like acquiring strength) requires work. I can acquire it "naturally"—meaning that in the course of daily life I place myself in situations that require equilibrium (such as cutting the high grass in the meadow with a scythe). My practice sessions on the wire are so much a part of my routine that they function that way for me. Or I can work "artificially" on my balance by doing exercises designed to improve it. Generally speaking, I detest such exercises, but the improvements they bring are both rapid and tangible.

In the spirit of which—and as an exception to my general aversion to books that offer exercises—I offer you this one, which I call *Find your foot-of-equilibrium and stand on one leg, eyes closed.* (A long title for a short exercise.)

Stand on a chair.

Which foot did you place first on the chair? If you didn't notice, come down and climb up again. This time, pay attention to which foot "naturally" starts the climbing motion. It's probably the same foot you always put forth when you begin walking or (especially) when you balance on one leg. From now on, call it your "foot-of-equilibrium."

Now stand, feet slightly apart and parallel, arms hanging naturally, eyes on the horizon—invent a horizon, if one is not readily available!—and close your eyes. (A word about this commonly invoked foot position: Bruce Lee deserves credit for discovering, through his extensive study and practice of martial arts, that it is the position that best allows a body balanced in the standing position to launch into any kind of action: the equilibrium at rest extends to the balance in motion.)

Remaining firmly grounded on your foot-of-equilibrium, lift the other knee until the thigh of that leg is horizontal. Holding that position, count the seconds—*real* seconds, "One-potato, two-potato, three-potato . . ." until you start to lose your balance and are forced to open your eyes.

What's your number?

One to three is not bad.

Four to six is good.

Above seven is excellent.

Now try with the other leg.

Repeat this exercise daily and monitor your progress.

If I am able to balance blindly on one leg for thirty seconds, sometimes longer, it is thanks to a life of balance on steel cables and hemp ropes. I recently calculated that the distance I've walked during all my performances and all my practice sessions adds up to some 40,000 kilometers on the high wire, which (as I forgot to remember from second grade) is roughly the circumference of the Earth!

You can tell I'm not opposed to cultivating balance.

But then I feel I never have enough of it.

The hidden face of balance

What I find interesting is the face of balance that hides its face.

If I want two carpentry vises to secure a piece of wood, I'll tighten their handles simultaneously, using both hands at once. This is an exercise in opposed symmetry—each hand turns each screw in the same direction. It is also an exercise in ambidexterity—which is an illustration of that hidden face of balance.

Such subtle balance adds to my abilities, it strengthens my overall demeanor.

So break the bad habit of serving balance with a predominant foot or hand! Reserve your foot-of-equilibrium (and your "good" hand) for emergency situations or when time is of the essence.

Give all you have to balance. That is, use both of your feet equally and both of your hands equally. This is nature's original gift to man—I mean, have you ever heard of a left-handed chimpanzee?

Wait—this is not accurate.

In the wild, chimps are ambidextrous when performing difficult or large tasks. For smaller, finer jobs, they have hand preferences. And in captivity, chimps generally favor one hand over the other. (Is it because they observe and imitate their human captor's behavior?) So make like a wild chimp and try as much as possible to privilege all your limbs.

Life without balance

I say this not only because I am a high-wire artist.

I say it because it's true.

Balance, the bond that seals body to mind, is as essential to life as air and water. We cannot live without balance.

There are two kinds of people (take a guess which of the two I am): those who would leave a picture frame on a wall in their home hanging slightly off balance all year long and those who would stand up in the middle of dinner, interrupting conversation, and adjust it. (I say nothing about the fact that it was hanging askew in the first place—that is caused by minuscule vibrations of the building as it adjusts its own equilibrium!)

At a signing for my book *Man on Wire*, a person named Ariel (the name of the first aerial steam carriage) whispered to me, "You must be a man of extraordinary contradictions to have such good balance!"

"Yes and no!" was my modest reply.

Now put on your gloves and helmet and get ready for the next chapter . . .

No, you don't need a shield. Not yet.

((((((the secrets of bullfighting))))))

Territory is a three-dimensional detail!

A very important notion that animals live and survive by. That humans still use but have long forgotten exists.

Like any animal, mark your territory with details—embrace it as your life and be ready to defend it with your life.

One of the secrets of bullfighting has to do exactly with this concept.

An apprentice bullfighter at eighteen, I once served as *mozo de espada* (literally, "valet of the sword"—the bullfighter's assistant and confidant) to a young torero who taught me to observe the bull intently from the moment it springs out of the *toril*, the narrow, dark area where it has been kept captive for a few days.

The bull encounters a never-before-seen sight. It runs around briefly to explore the entire sandy arena. Here and there it stops; it runs again and stops.

In less than a minute, the animal will select a *querencia*, a small area where it likes to rest and where it feels strong enough to defy its adversaries. But it does not stay there; it bursts out of that area each time the torero provokes it to attack.

If the man inserts himself between the animal and its *querencia*, he is "trespassing" in the terrain of the bull, who might charge by surprise to clear its retreat route to the *querencia*, randomly swiping with rage at anything it encounters in its path.

This trespassing is the secret to accelerating the animal's charge, an acceleration that is essential for the successful execution of certain passes with the *muleta* (small cape), and definitely for the accurate placement of the *banderillas* (the short spears that must be planted in the neck of the bull to force it to lower its head in preparation for the moment of death).

Regardless of the project I pursue, when I reach my field of action, when it is time for me "to take the bull by the horns," I position myself in such a way as to profit from the brutal—yet frank—full force of the charge!

In my heart, there is no doubt.

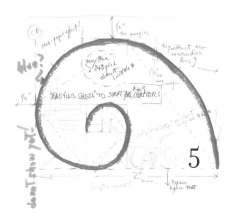

5 CRIMINAL PRACTICE

Dealing onto the table of the last chapter my notions about the many subversive elements that contribute to a successful coup, I stole a card! A card with details that, if played with repeatedly, sets the foundation of an art.

Here it is: when architect-engineers draw up the final blueprint for a building, they add detailed sections and elevations that show, for instance, how a girder connects to a joist.

(Hold on a second! Did you ever notice that in English, *engineer* comes from *engine*—the powering machine in a mechanical system; while in French, *ingénieur* derives from *génie*—the genius in human thinking?)

Structural details allow architectural details to exist and make construction possible. In the same manner, for three-dimensional concepts to generate art, they must be turned into an action, repeated a hundred-million times.

Take juggling, for example.

When I invent a new move, I gather its details and then give them life by working on them again and again. This process of repetition—which I have done for nearly sixty years—became the most important aspect of my performing apprenticeship. To grasp his art, to succeed, the juggler *needs* to put his juggling props into flight constantly and repeatedly.

Practice

Papa Rudy called it *la prax*: I had the expression embroidered in red onto the large white canvas bag I carry daily to practice.

I "invented" juggling (originally *to invent* meant to find out, to discover) by practicing with three potatoes of different sizes and shapes in a cold, humid, dimly lit basement filled with dusty archives and broken furniture.

The first day I could not even practice; I was busy clearing my workspace.

A month later, I shoplifted from a pet store three multicolored dog balls of hard rubber, three inches in diameter. They were heavy and rough in shape. I had to clean them every day and paint them flat-white every week.

It would be twenty years before I switched to three perfectly molded, very expensive white silicon balls with invisible seams. They're the perfect weight for my type of juggling, and they're maintenance-free.

From the instant I decided to make playing cards disappear, juggling clubs fly, and wire-ropes support my aerial promenades, I repeated the same moves again and again and again. For years. Sometimes all day. Even today.

Let's look into the chemistry of such madness.

My dialogue with objects during practice

I can still remember how I learned to do a difficult juggling move—throwing a ball above my head and catching it behind my back, the sort of move jugglers call a *blind trick*.

Despite my undivided attention, the first hundred attempts failed magnificently. Most people would have given up at that point. Intuitively, I knew that if I continued duplicating the same attempt another hundred times—mechanically, passively—success would depend only on luck, and that was unacceptable to me.

It was clear that in order to learn the move, I needed to understand the move. And that instead of using only my hands, like a robot, I had to bring in my soul.

At first, for some time, the ball was hitting the nape of my neck on the way down. In a natural but pernicious reflex, I was ducking my head slightly forward to avoid being hit by the hard little ball.

I was unable to eliminate that reflex until I decomposed the throw in imaginary slow motion and discovered the cause: I wasn't throwing the ball high enough, which was creating an urgency about catching it. The throw-and-catch sequence was too short and too rapid for me to control.

I started throwing the ball quite high, which added an element of drama to its flight and allowed me to keep an eye on the vertical axis of its descent. The result? The ball cleared the back of my neck each time! But the open hand positioned against my lower back kept missing the catch.

I caught the solution red-handed when I transformed myself into the flying object.

As the ball, I had no difficulty correcting my *own* midair trajectory. I saw that I had been drawing an arc when I should have been following a path straight up and down. Once I aligned my axis of descent with the center of the juggler's nape, I fell precisely along the center of the juggler's back and landed in his waiting hand for a perfect catch. Each time!

From being the ball, I transformed back into being the juggler. Now that I had acquired this delicate juggling move, all I had to do was work hard to master it. Then work harder to perfect it.

I'd refine part of a movement for hours, adding a flourish to the beginning or stretching the ellipsis of its ending. I might also search for novel combinations. I might marry speed and slow motion. I might choreograph suspensions.

Then something strange would happen.

As soon as I reached mastery of a movement and had put it aside to work on something else, the movement I had just perfected—with no warning—went on vacation! It eluded me and refused to return.

I had to recall the culprit at each of my daily sessions and spend time relearning it—that is, repracticing it. Once I had repracticed a move—even the most difficult—it never escaped again.

This is the reason I have in my pocket at all times the Maria Theresa silver coin my friend the director Werner Herzog offered me long ago: so that I can practice my magic manipulations almost constantly.

In my early years of apprenticeship, I repeated a movement to learn it. Today, I repeat it to hold on to what I've learned. In the process, I am rewarded with an unending elation: the pleasure of dialoguing with my props, which have become so much more than indispensable professional tools since I am convinced that their prowess manifests itself only once they've become an extension of my body and my mind. In this communion, we become one.

Before I ask my battered black street-juggling top hat (made from a single piece of leather) to do "hat moves" with me during practice, I wake it up gently by twirling it briefly around my thumb and landing its rim flat on the bed of my horizontal, folded right arm in an ancient salute W. C. Fields used to execute in his films (a move Papa Rudy described as "to make a compliment").

I do the same with each of my props before I start working with them: I bring them to life with a little welcoming move, an invitation-to-motion that I call *salut à l'objet*, which you could translate as "greeting the prop."

At the beginning of a juggling workshop, I always allow each student a few minutes to come up with a decidedly personal "silly little move" with which to gently wake up the object they are about to dialogue with.

Before I write, I spin my pen across my fingers; before I draw, I line up my pencils in order of graphic intensity; before I cut wood with my chisel, I send the mallet into the air—double somersault!—and catch it.

One day I stood five feet away from world-champion chess player Boris Spassky as he began a multiplayer simultaneous tournament. Before his first move, I saw him adjust his and his opponent's pieces very quickly on the board. Was it to ensure that they all remained under his spell?

Before you do your first move, before you leave the spell of this chapter and search and borrow and design your own *prax* . . . I should talk about something I know nothing of: practicing other arts than the ones that inhabit me!

But wait! Whatever your field of artistry, whatever training you have adopted in your daily life—whether you are a sculptor, a dancer, an athlete—you need to submit to physical repetition in order to progress. And I would be remiss if I were not to advocate loud and clear that when it comes to training, "crisscrossing" arts is a good idea. Physical exercises from one art will improve your thinking in another as surely as thoughts from one art will empower the physicality of the other.

Throughout my life I have crisscrossed my arts in exactly this way, even though I rarely admit it. For example, I "train" as a writer with the methods of the barn builder, the exercises of the lock-picking master, and the reflexes of the juggler . . .

My last words on the subject:

Go to school if you want to learn.

Go to life if you want to feel.

But whatever you do, never ever end practice on a failure. It's a sure way to catch the deadly disease of lethargy!

How to rest

On my wall I have a visual reminder that resting can be harmonious: Charles Ebbets's iconic photograph of construction workers taking a lunch break from their work on the RCA Building at Rockefeller Center in 1932. Sitting side by side on a long steel I-beam suspended eight hundred feet above the sidewalks of Manhattan, they rest.*

I came up with a theory about resting—that specific moment when fatigue should no longer be fought, when I should allow myself a break, because even the fanatic, passionate and impatient artist *must* rest; that's a given. (Although when a friend helping me in a building task asks for time to rest, I say, "Sure!" but secretly think, *What a waste of time!*)

---

*Taken on September 20, 1932 (© Bettmann/Corbis).

My concept of resting is to invite your props or tools to rest with you.

Let's say you have been timber-framing all morning. The handles of your mallet and your chisel have warmed up to your hands, melded with the inside of your palms, become a cog in the mechanism of your wrists; they have become an extension of yourself.

You decide to rest a bit—to light a cigarette, to take a sip of red wine, to strike up a conversation with a friend—and so you put chisel and mallet back in the toolbox. The second your fingers abandon the tool, the chisel returns to cold steel; the mallet goes back to being a mere wooden assembly, as if awaiting a customer in a store window. You have abandoned them, they now abandon you. They are the tools of someone else. Or of no one.

After hours of high-wire practice, to let the fatigue evaporate, sometimes I sit in the middle of the cable, facing the platform; I bend forward, lean both forearms on the cable, and rest my head on them. (I call this position "potato" because it lacks elegance.) Or else, I sit perpendicular to the axis of the cable and face away from it. (I call this the "bird" because that's how birds perch on electric lines along our roads.) At times I even lie down on the wire and close my eyes. I do any of these things rather than return to the platform, secure my balancing-pole, change shoes, and walk away from the wire. By resting *on the cable*, I hold on to the balance I created earlier and keep the wire warm with the conversation we were having before I surrendered to resting.

Even if I merely need to put on a new CD in the middle of practicing my three-balls juggling routine, without a thought I'll hook two balls under one arm and lock the third under my chin to free both hands instead of setting the props on the table.

To let go of the tools of your trade, to exit the theater of your creation during a pause, is to annihilate the entire meaningful alchemy you have created in your practice.

Tools or props, I keep them on me when I rest. On me? In me as well. One time while building the barn, I stopped for lunch but decided not to wash my hands. I wanted the smell of the wood to add flavor to my pear and Roquefort sandwich. As I licked my fingers, I inadvertently swallowed sawdust, as if the trees were feeding back to me the timber I had been cutting from them!

One day I really upset Francis Brunn! He saw me packing my suitcase after a show, in preparation for checking out of our hotel. For a moment I laid on the bed my juggling clubs and the ball and hoops my friend had just given me. He held my arm and sharply told me of the tradition—should I say superstition?—among performers that props should never be put on a bed.

"And why is that?" I asked.

"Well," the legendary juggler informed me, "they might fall asleep!"

But what about the props that have served for too long, that are battered beyond use? Should they be put to sleep? No! Ultimately, they need to retire. When it's that time for my props, I put them all to rest in special places.

My regular top hats (prior to the leather one), all inscribed with their period of usage, used to hang side by side from the rafters of Rue Laplace until I was forced to abandon the place. Today they still hang—but now dispersed all over the world—from the ceilings of friends' homes. My leather hat will one day go to endless sleep into the same custom-made box I manufactured long ago for its numerous travels.

The white balls (I have so many of them) glide into a cylindrical transparent tube that accepts only three of them, so at a glance I can tell they're all there—as if ready to go back into play!

My collection of juggling clubs? Each one is held vertically by a circular clasp screwed into the edge of a girt in the barn. Next to them, my hoops, always in sets of six, hang on flat hooks wide enough to not weaken their plastic flesh.

"Good night, good life, and good afterlife!" I bid them.

Everyday

I practice every day.

Which is probably the reason why the habit of performing certain actions on a daily basis appeals to me. I do not think of them as discipline exercises (even if they are), but as entertaining interruptions in my hectic way of devouring the day.

A long time ago, newly (and unlawfully) installed in the Parisian broom-closet I would call home for the next forty-five years, I decided to hone my three-ball juggling routine. Impatient for progress, eager to reach the next slab of time for practicing other disciplines, I came up with a daily ritual.

Every morning, the instant I woke up, I forced myself to go through—only once—the first thirty seconds of my five-minute routine (the remainder would follow later in the day). My fingers and my eyes, barely awake—therefore not yet communicating—had to double their attention to keep the balls in flight. But the strenuous process forced this brief *juggling-intro* to penetrate my body and infiltrate my soul.

Not only did my fingers gain independence and my sense of touch improve, but also I quickly learned by heart the complicated succession of moves.

A year later, I don't know why, I asked Francis Brunn to give me six of his white hoops. He did.

Oh, I know why! So I could spice up my practice sessions with a dash of the impossible . . . since it was clear to me that I would never be able to juggle them as fast, as fluidly, and as long as my friend—my best friend.

At the same time that I added the six hoops to the very end of my already overloaded self-apprenticeship program, I monitored my meager progress with another childish procedure. Each time I was able (by miracle) to throw and catch the six hoops (I called that "doing one exchange"), I glued to the frame of the giant mirror above the bed one of those little white rings used to reinforce the holes of perforated pages. The satisfaction of witnessing my progress at a glance, as well as the anticipation of one day seeing the frame completely covered with little rings, had me quite excited and persuaded me to keep trying (almost against all odds) every day.

Two years later, I peeled off hundreds of tiny rings from the entirely covered frame and threw them in the garbage. My new challenge with the large hoops was now to make as many exchanges in a row as possible.

A short while thereafter, I stopped gluing tiny rings to mirror frames; wisdom finally had me abandon self-competition. It was more intelligent to concentrate with all my might on the work rather than to continue the game of breaking my own records—which actually concerned solely the technique I was acquiring—not the art of juggling.

But another early habit persists today.

Whenever I grab three, four or five citrus fruits to make juice at breakfast, I must—I *must*—juggle them for a few seconds! In the other room, Kathy can now tell by the occasional sound of fruit dropping that a delicious fresh-squeezed beverage is on its way.

When?

It happens every day!

A decade or so ago, aging got me thinking that working deliberately to maintain the physical strength of my youth might not be a bad idea. It was. Physical strength dilutes as we age. It can't be maintained at a youthful level as one grows old; it needs to be reconsidered.

I was inspired by Bruce Lee. In his memoir *Tao of Jeet Kune Do*, he tells how he developed his obsession of exercising his body every day, all day, every possible moment of the day. One evening when he was watching television, he realized his body was just sitting there. He quickly added some wrist-and-ankle-strengthening-moves he could soon perform unconsciously, without distracting his viewing.

In this spirit, I hung a flying trapeze—destined to remain unflying forever—from the ceiling of my basement. I made a vow to do the longest series of pull-ups I could each time I passed under the trapeze. Since the bar hangs at the bottom of the stairs leading to my workbench and to my desk, which I visit many times a day, it proved to be a great incentive to keep strong.

The importance of a journal

To keep track of the training of the props—as well as my own training—and to record our ongoing exchange, I jot down our mutual daily progress inside a little notebook that usually lasts a year.

Dozens of these *prax*-diaries—which I call *dailies*, each dedicated exclusively to juggling or the high wire—adorn a long shelf in my archive room.

A typical entry carries the date with a little pictogram indicating the weather (a sun, a cloud—sometimes strong wind, rain or snow).

I divide the practice into specialized work periods: exercises with the hat; the large ball; the six hoops; the three balls; other props; and I record the time spent working on each.

The repetitive part of the practice session, when I try again and again a difficult move with a specific prop—until I'm satisfied with the number of

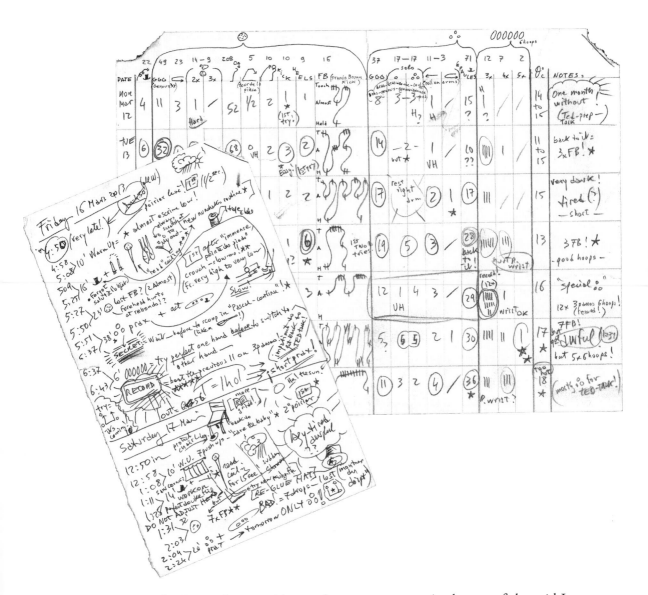

"victories"—I record on a grid spread over two pages. At the top of the grid I have a line of little frames, each housing a tiny hieroglyph symbolizing the move. Just above that, in pencil, I've marked my own "world record" to date for each of the moves! Breaking such a record triggers a scream of joy and calls for celebration!

In addition, aside from the grid, I jot down whatever makes the session an unusual one.

Sometimes, on an impulse to break the monotony of my system, I eliminate the tracking of Time. But if I take the time to eliminate Time, I haven't won the Time game! Yes, whenever I do not record the time spent to work each specialized section of a practice session, I feel dangerously free. But it never lasts long. On the next day, I go back to my usual time-logging—the only way I know to monitor my work all year long.

When I discover the secret to the successful execution of a particularly elusive movement (circus people use the word *trick*—I can't), I write in bold "**Secret =** " and explain to myself in writing—for posterity—what triggered the victory.

When I discover a new exercise or a subtle move I've never done before—a different kind of victory—I proudly inscribe "**1st**" inside a little square and fill it with an orange highlight (nothing stands out better!).

Are "firsts" rare?

No!

Sometimes I flip through my most recent *dailies* just to be encouraged by the frequency of the little orange squares. Over the course of a week, it is not unusual for me to find one per day or more, even dozens a week—my kind of week! You think I'm gloating? No, I'm just sharing the hidden wonders that *la prax* brings!

Athletes who train for the Olympic Games develop their own detailed means of following their progress (and noticing periods of plateau) by monitoring their daily training in some sort of written log. Otherwise, how could a master swimmer take aim at cutting those precious fractions of a second that make a world record?

Sometimes, when I feel the need, I introduce as a creative challenge a difficult, uncalled-for task that I simply decide I must perform each and every day—or else feel I have failed.

For example, from an Australian tour I brought back a wordless little book labeled *365*. It has a bold number printed at the top of each of its three hundred sixty-five blank pages. As an exercise for my writing, starting with page one on January first, I decided to make one literary entry each day—a brief observation, a quote I'd encountered recently, a fifty-five-word story,* a tiny poem . . . The discipline this daily exercise demands surprised me—some days I have to force myself just to uncap my fountain pen and open the book.

Some of my daily habits of practice you might find naive or silly, but their aim and result are utterly serious: they develop the focus and discipline any successful artistic coup demands.

Focus and discipline

When I present a complex card routine at a close-up table at the Magic Castle; when I tailor my juggling act to a musical improvisation by my friend the composer J. Ralph, seated at his Blüthner grand piano; when, balancing-pole in hand, I step out of the gothic arch high above the nave of the Cathedral of St. John the Divine to perform my first (and illegal) high-wire

---

*Inspired by *The World's Shortest Stories*, a compilation of short stories just fifty-five words long, edited by Steve Moss (Philadelphia: Running Press, 1998).

crossing there . . . I become possessed by a rare, otherworldly sense that instantly increases my energy, strengthens my body and soul, and protects my life—a sense that defies analysis, resists teaching and—if I'm not holding on to it—evaporates surprisingly fast: *focus.*

The focus that allows me to reach beyond my normal abilities, that cloaks my frequent intrusions into the domain of the impossible, comes from a life-long complicity with concentration.

I can't offer a formula for developing focus. But I know how it developed for me.

In my youth, I thought that the concentration needed to teach myself any number of arts derived from rejecting the world around. How naive! The focus thus created was like a funnel whose opening was half plugged. On the narrow end, my progress emerged, drop by distilled drop, tasting sharp and concentrated; but on the receiving end, the world could not pour in freely.

My system lacked the subtlety and flexibility I needed to progress into the sophisticated artist I was learning to become. As I honed my craft through decades of practicing, rehearsing and performing, I learned—first consciously, and then unconsciously—to refine the nature of my focus. I came to vary my method with my mood and with the activity I was trying to master. And it continued to evolve.

Today, the constant is the contradictory state in which I place myself: *I ignore the entire world while listening to the entire world.*

It works!

For instance, when I'm on the high wire, I am capable of filtering all of my incoming thoughts: a joyful childhood memory will be allowed to pass, what I will have for dinner that night will not.

My simultaneously ignoring/listening focus also heightens my senses ten-fold. The peripheral range of my vision expands: I may notice someone from the audience stepping inside the forbidden security perimeter—under the wire— even if it happens almost behind me. I can catch a faint whiff of burning in the distance (for a crossing guy-lined by dry hemp ropes, this might prove to be an important piece of information!). My tactile sensitivity is especially acute: with my toes, I can feel the tiniest vibrations in the cable if an assistant adjusts the tensioning device. An uneducated spectator might think that the sense of taste has nothing to do with wire-walking. But I discreetly chew the air I traverse, which allows my tongue to measure the degree of humidity. Once, after starting a long crossing, I could tell it was about to rain; I accelerated my pace and reached arrival just before a sudden downpour!

It takes discipline to focus like that.*

In my daily life, I make humbleness and daring tenacity meet by exercising constant discipline, in the form of rules I have trained myself to follow.

Some of these are not so easy for someone who is eternally running out of time! Take, for instance, the pledge I made to repair an item the minute it's broken. It's not such a silly goal—when you need to use a rake is not the time to replace its broken handle. Then why are two baskets brimming with things to be fixed looking at me for the past two years? If this were a how-to manual on creativity, I would throw at you tons of other rules for daily life that help instill discipline; but it's not. Thus I invite you to make up your own.

*See Miyoko Shida assemble an ephemeral mobile with utmost "disciplined focus" at Flixxy.com.

Play attention

Yes, *play*.

Were your eyes deceived? Did your brain correct the heading to *Pay attention*? If so, it is time for you to pull out of your skull the minuscule "spell check" chip and throw it back at my fiend (not *friend*) the computer!

Let it stand: I *play* with my attention during practice.

Within the same exercise, I experiment with varying the kind of focus the work depends upon.

I invite all my senses to gather and mingle in order to serve my creativity in the most surprising and efficient manner. I set myself into a state of *wild openness*. By the way, **what's wrong with our senses?** Are they like wild animals in danger of extinction?

Yesterday, in the middle of the wire, as I was gliding step by step in slow motion—the most demanding way to walk—I abruptly stopped. A thought about this book had to be jotted down before it evaporated, which I did sitting on the cable near the departure platform!

On the ground sometimes, I'll lock myself inside the tiniest of cells, that of my ultimate intense focus (usually reserved for the wire), and this time, unbeknownst to me, imperceptibly I'll metamorphose again into whatever prop I'm handling!

Paying attention is fine. But the seriousness it entails will rarely allow for uncommon intellectual detours, for mental *démultiplication* (a French automotive term meaning "reduction in gear ratio," but used by poets—and as such, it has no equivalent in English) and various other chance encounters that a state of playfulness (or openness) often offers. So when you have to pay utmost attention, try adding a pinch of naiveté or try smiling at the same time!

Personally, if I were hanging by one hand to a cliff, I would think that cracking a joke, or at least allowing a funny thought to reach me, might contribute to my recovery: humor definitely carries enormous positive force!

In any case, try to expand your mental horizon.

Let's be more serious.

Imagine you are in a survival situation. Life is at stake. Minutes count. If you face such adversity with only a selection from which your personality is composed, I believe you might not survive. To empower yourself, to save your life, you must draw from all that you're made of and all that you did not know you had in you—anything positive (rage and rebellion are fine; panic and despair are not). Then you will save your life.

Stress may invite creativity! As Gene Hackman, playing a commanding officer in the submarine drama *Crimson Tide*, answers the critique of a fellow officer: "On the other hand, *I* believe that to conduct a drill while there is a fire on board is the best way to prepare my men for . . ."

Creative paranoia

As an author, when I scribble my first drafts, I do not allow a thesaurus on the desk. I find it dangerously wrong (although very tempting) to polish a paragraph before the raw thought has had time to sizzle. Not allowing that reference tool near my fingertips muffles my author's impatience (which I confess often prevents me from thinking calmly); it's a shield against my confrontation with Time.

This is one subtle way I've found to protect against my pernicious inclination to reach a goal as directly and quickly as I can.

I exercise "creative paranoia" in other ways too, to protect and respect both the process of invention and the process of refinement. For example, I color-code my first drafts: red means "not a perfect choice of word—to improve later" (but not now when it might derail my train of thought); blue signifies an example to be found or described at length; brown shows a topic to develop; and black, like indelible China ink, means "text to stay."

These may seem like random preferences or inconsequential systems to you, but they work for me. And I'll add to them any method, simple or sophisticated, that has the power to diffuse the tension that constantly attempts to interrupt the flow of creativity.

So should you.

The same vigilance I exercise with respect to my process governs my choice of implements. The wrong writing tool would merely heighten my creative paranoia. Once the beloved sepia ink of my first draft has dried, it is time to transfer my words to the computer.

Alas, we are not on friendly terms.

The evil machine accepts "yes" and "no" only in the form of *enter* and *delete*, when what I wish for is a *maybe* option. And there are always three different ways to send a command instead of only one: the fastest, simplest, most logical.

With the premonition that the computer might win, I try not to start an argument.

Another favorite way to go forward in my creative practice: anticipate.

I foresee obstacles and ways of bypassing them—then I imagine the unforeseen and improvise how to deal with it!

Invite Murphy to dinner. (Of course, something will happen at the last minute, and he'll cancel. Ha!)

But don't waste your time rehearsing the general's speech before the battle; instead, make sure your troops show up.

And depending on your inklings, leave nothing to chance—or as little as possible.

Does ambivalence belong to "creative paranoia"?

Well, again . . . yes and no!

Use your creative paranoia to be on the lookout for negativity; observe with a positive spirit: "What a beautiful disaster!" uttered the French architect Le Corbusier when he visited Manhattan for the first time.

Transform negative into positive: "What is a weed? A weed is a plant whose virtues have not been discovered," wrote Ralph Waldo Emerson.

I would be remiss if I did not mention that along my creative path, here and there, rise clusters of "paranoia trees" (whose fruits, evidently, are sweet-and-sour). They shade me from the burning sun of relentless invention, which everyone knows can lead to intellectual exhaustion or, worse, inventing the wrong way. By imposing a delay, by offering a pause, they temper my ardor to rush forward and sometimes that allows me to glance ahead at the ground and notice the nail about to pierce my foot!

Moderation with excess

At the risk of startling you, I'll interject: consider all that you've read so far as open to variation, as ripe for contradiction! Think "moderation with excess."

Oh, I could write about excess for forty days and forty nights!

At *excess*, my quotation dictionary offers this from Le Duc de Saint-Simon. (If you don't know who he was, Google him!) "Let's run away from the insanity of extremities, they only lead to the abyss!"

No-no-no-no-no!

Let's multiply the insanity of extremities. Let's collect the abysses!

Talking about excess . . .

I suspect my discourse in this chapter—daily exercises and all—has been demanding for you as well.

Are you as exhausted as I?

By inviting you into my creative laboratory to witness relentless trials and efforts, I hope I have made you more aware of the necessary independence, the loneliness of the creative outlaw, and of the countless obstacles and hazards that confront the perfect crime. This is excellent preparation for our next chapter, in which, thanks to intensive effort, THE PLOT THICKENS.

((((what's wrong with our senses?))))

We've limited them to five.
We seldom use all of them equally.
We rarely exercise them fully.
We almost never combine them.
That's what's wrong.

In order to toss my juggling hat onto my head or execute difficult moves with it, I must know at all times where the front and the back of it are; they happen to look alike, but the hat only fits my head one way: the back in the back.

So I glued a little white dot on the inner seam of the back. Now, in a fraction of a glimpse, I can check which side of the hat I am holding. Or if my eyes are otherwise not available, I can feel the slight thickness of the dot with my fingertips!

Yes, like me, you can grow little eyes at the tips of your fingers.

No one teaches us this, but we can interchange our senses, overlap or combine them. Marry two senses, and a new one will soon be born.

Animals do this instinctively; we, no longer. They follow nature's laws, relying on sight, hearing, smell, touch and taste, while we humans have become expert at forgetting our instinctive-intuitive behavior.

The most recurrent line in police accident reports reads "They looked but did not see."

Here is a story about seeing without looking.

Upon my return to the Catskills from a winter journey, my neighbor TJ gives me the seasonal warning: "Be careful, the bear is back!"

Armed only with a walking stick and Werner Herzog's advice ("If confronted by a bear, scream Bavarian insults at the top of your lungs and show your teeth!"), I step into the thick woods.

I am looking for a sapling to replace the handle of my cant hook.

I look for the right tree. I observe while walking, I stop to glance around, I look, I look . . .

But for the bear, *looking* is not enough! I know that scanning from side to side will not help me spot a predator if it decides to "play dead," to hold its life in suspension in order to become invisible.

For me to see the bear, I must not look. I must use some of what master trackers refer to as "splatter vision" or "soft-focus eyes" (once voluntarily unfocused, the eyes exercise more peripheral vision) and also what I call "sensefulness," which consists of blending all my senses evenly and using the result as one new sense!

In one word, I must *perceive* the animal's *presence*.

I advance on a soft bed of dead leaves, silent, trying not to breathe, and find myself in a state of walking awareness.

You see, I'm returning to an animal state.

Bruce Lee in *Enter the Dragon* (a film of otherwise less-than-stellar quality) does not need to turn around to take in his chain-wielding assailants or to appraise their lethal determination. Instead, half man, half leopard, he lowers his gaze and widens his inner eyes, gauging the thugs with all his senses. My fascination for his balletic fighting resides in the fact that he does not overtly watch the action, he seems to orchestrate it from inside a fort of sentient self-confidence.

That's exactly how I felt from the moment I set foot inside the freight elevator the evening before my WTC coup, until just minutes before stepping on the wire. To fight adversity, to improvise, to solve problems, and to save the coup, I had gathered all my senses into unusual configurations, which made me grow wild and enhanced my perceptions.

The perfect example of this elusive yet powerful chemistry is the incident I recall as *Pas de deux*.

Just as darkness is about to give way to dawn's gleam, a guard comes to the roof of the tower where my friend Jean-François and I are rigging the cable. Fortunately, the static of his walkie-talkie gives me a five-second warning.

I signal my accomplice to lie flat, but I am caught near the center of the roof, with nowhere to hide. I must stand behind a pile of rubbish and hope for the best.

The guard pauses on one side of the pile; I stand on the other.

He walks around the pile. So do I.

He stops. I stop.

He keeps circling. So do I.

He finally leaves. I stay!

This little *pas de deux* could have been fatal to the coup, if I had not transformed into a wildcat, relying on pure instinct and letting my senses overlap and mingle.

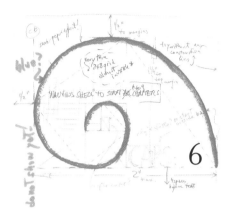

6 | THE PLOT THICKENS

During my months and months of preparations for my walk at the World Trade Center, a thorough review of the information I had jotted in my *cahier* had yielded "the plan" that became the backbone of my "WTC operation."

That plan, painstakingly improved through much trial and error, had empowered me all along. It gave me the courage to keep fighting the impossible; it made me arrive with strength and certitude to the day of the coup.

But once inside the towers, I discarded most of its components in favor of sheer improvisation triggered by intuition . . . and, yes, by chance.

Strange as it seems, I became truly fortified by the plan only when I had the courage to alter it, to give it a fresh new spin. (That was during the first phase of the coup, right as I stepped inside the freight elevator!)

So I plan—obsessively. (You should see how I prepare for my "improvised" lectures!) In fact, the essence of my creativity resides mainly in my preparations, as I force my art crime to shape up. But I plan . . . *mmhh* . . . let's say . . . creatively!

Is my master plan my master?

When I plan any wire-walk, I construct a scale model. The plan for my illegal walk at Notre Dame took shape inside my head over the hours in which I meticulously assembled my model. As I added details, I solved problems and came up with new ideas. In a sense, the three-dimensional model not only feeds the plan in my head, it *becomes* the plan.

But even when there isn't a scale model, no matter what coup I'm plotting, my master plan—heart and soul of the crime—proves three-dimensional.

At first, as I described in Chapter 2, you gather notions that are strangers to each other. Like humans, the more they grow in number, the more they congregate into groups of affinity and form clans. As you brainstorm further connections, like humans they continue to conspire (they plot their survival!) . . . and before you know it, the shadow of a plan emerges. Give this intellectual selection enough time, and an entire course of action surfaces. Aggrandized by the result, you will feel as if you had engineered it!

Actually, it's not that there is a plan on one side and chance on the other. The plan itself is a living organism that, when nurtured carefully and under the right conditions, gives birth to an entire creative process that includes the benefits of the serendipitous.

Everything that we need to accomplish our artistic crime is already etched in the watermark of the blueprint we've drafted! Plan—and through the act of planning, sooner or later, all your relevant questions will be addressed and answered—along with all the necessary details.

A plan frees details

During World War II, a group of daring French officers held captive at the Oflag XVII-A, a prison camp somewhere in northern Germany—my father was one of them—pulled off a daring mass escape (one hundred and forty officers), following months of secret planning and tunnel digging (which—amazingly—they recorded with a concealed 8mm camera). The adventure became a documentary, *Sous le Manteau* (Under the Cloak)—sadly in need of restoration so it can be made available again!—and helped inspire the feature film *The Great Escape*.

Something in particular fascinated me.

As the guards kept an eye on the camp from their watchtowers, they witnessed the same boring image day after day, month after month: dozens of wooden barracks standing right next to one another. In front of them, hundreds of prisoners continually walked by. As I said, boring.

Here's what they did not see.

The prisoners planning the escape were in desperate need of wooden planks to prevent the tunnel they were digging from collapsing. They managed to steal boards from different structures in the camp, some of them quite long. But how could they transport this precious loot across the camp without being caught, which would mean delays in the tunnel work as well as severe reprisals?

Their solution was ingenious: a length of twine was tied to each end of the plank resting on the ground. A prisoner picked up the free end of each piece of twine and wrapped it around his hand until the plank, still horizontal, lifted an inch off the ground. Then the pair of them walked unhurriedly alongside the barracks, their arms swinging naturally, exactly as if they were promenading empty-handed. From a distance, only a highly motivated observer could have caught the anomaly: what seemed to be the bottom plank of a barracks wall was indeed traveling in pace with the strolling prisoners!

I employed this genius concept while preparing for my illegal walk at the Sydney Harbor Bridge in 1973. The night before, I had to carry my twenty-five-foot-long balancing-pole from the access-road entrance to the pylon I had broken into. Three hundred yards of exposed sidewalk, with police cars cruising by regularly! My criminal mind convinced me that two guys carrying a long white pipe would look suspicious.

Just like those prisoners, my accomplice and I made our way along the sidewalk, me in the lead, my friend twenty feet behind. Suspended from our arms, the long pipe made its way with us, hovering an inch above the gutter. We had practiced how to swing our arms, to acquire the barely perceptible, natural arm-swinging that would not betray our action: passing drivers saw only two independent fellows crossing the bridge empty-handed.

Details save my life, I think constantly when I am preparing for a high-wire walk.

In a "live rigging system," that is, one that includes parts in motion (such as a cable traveling through the sheaves of a tensioning device), it is essential to secure the pins of all shackles to prevent them from being shaken loose (invisibly!) by vibrations.

Details of this sort, but also details in general, I find to be the lifeblood of any artistic crime. The tool, the instrument, the prop, has to suit the performer to the last detail. The artist, intellectually as well as physically, will sometimes die or live by such details.

For example, because he was left-handed, Charlie Chaplin had his violin and cello modified—the bass bar and sound post repositioned, and numerous other alterations, at great expense—so that he could play them "from the opposite side."

Sometimes accident—literally—forces an attention to detail that results in complete innovation.

After losing his right hand in a car accident at the age of nine, the young Argentinean René Lavand decided to learn magic.* He had to do so completely on his own, however, because all the existing techniques had been developed for two-handed magicians. By the age of thirty-two, he began to tour the world. His specialty was a close-up performance, which included an unusual style of misdirection and a unique type of manipulation he had developed, often advertised as *lentidigitation* (literally, "slow finger work," as distinct from the usual speedy *prestidigitation*).

One evening, surrounded by thoroughly mystified professional magicians—the most demanding audience for an illusionist—he concluded a brilliant demonstration by whispering, as if it were a mere detail, "What I just did, my friends, can also be achieved with two hands!"

The necessity of reinventing magic in its most minute detail—to plan it, in effect, from the ground up—had led to radical, enviable creativity.

Like many writers, I adore the detail in language itself, and I attend to it in zealous detail. For example, I love *aizuchi*, the minute expressions of interest with which the Japanese punctuate a conversation to let the speaker know that the listener is indeed listening (and understanding), and to encourage the speaker to keep on speaking: *Hai. Ee. Soo desu ka? Soo desu ne.*

When a Japanese storyteller is surrounded by a Japanese crowd, a soft rain of *aizuchi* begins to fall—such "sound-effects" can be hilarious to a Westerner's ears. Yet French has such expressions as well, and so does English: *Really? Yeah. Mm-hmm. No? Oh my! Aha.*

But language details aren't merely curiosities to collect. When I read, I tend

*Discover the life and work of this great artist-inventor in Lavand's *Mysteries of My Life* (with Richard Kaufman) and in *Magic from the Soul* (Pasadena, CA: Magic Words, 1993).

to trust a text that has its details right. And a lack of detail, I know, makes me distance myself from a piece of writing, even to disbelieve it.

Once, at a writing workshop, a student read the sentence "Then he poured himself a drink, and as he was drinking, he thought . . ."

"No," I interrupted him. "Paint your character, make us witness the action!"

Then I surprised him and the other aspiring writers by pulling a variety of drinking glasses out of a cardboard box.

I picked up a heavy mug with a thick handle and mimed pouring beer until the foam was about to overflow. I waited for it to subside, then grabbed the handle (my thumb on top of the rim for strength and balance) and brought the mug to my lips. "That's the regular way," I explained.

"But Germans tend to disregard the handle and smack their curved palm against the side of the mug, creating enough friction to lift it. However, Bavarians—for whom beer is a religion—hold the mug like this." I set the mug with the handle facing me and slid my fingers—but not my thumb—through the handle, palm turned toward me, away from the glass. Then I carefully lifted the mug off the table and tilted it slightly toward me so that the back of my hand supported its weight. I leaned my chin on my relaxed thumb and mimed drinking. "Purists don't look at the glass when drinking," I added. "They do not glance around—they do not tolerate the slightest distraction. They stare at the horizon and do not smile: beer drinking is a serious matter. Then they slam the empty mug on the table with a forceful *klunk* that can be heard from the other side of the hall!"

I had learned all this under the ear-splitting tent of a traditional German beerfest, from the most fanatic of all Bavarians, my ferocious friend Werner Herzog, who would not stop correcting my glance.

"Look at the *ho-rri-zon* for Christ's sake!"

"But I can't see the horizon, there is no horizon!"

"Invent the *ho-rri-zon*!"

Then I became a French sommelier. I poured a priceless Bordeaux into a tulip-shaped glass, twirling it to "breathe" the wine, admired the vertical lines (the *legs*) left by the alcohol on the glass's inner walls, and held it above my head to gauge the wine's color (the *robe*). I brought the rim to my nose to finish taking stock of all the qualities of this exceptional beverage before at last I splashed a little inside my mouth to put my taste buds to work—and then, at last, swallowed it.

I ended with a scene from a Russian party: guests drinking vodka in one gulp and throwing their empty glasses over the left shoulder!

"You see," I said, "if in just a few words you had described the drinking, you would have brought life to the character and the scene."

As a wire-walker does, a writer *survives* by details. This book, for example, is made of details. And what is a story but a sequence of details?

And yet, before I leave the topic of planning—speaking as the paranoid, over-organized, yet rebellious poet that I am—I would be remiss if I did not acknowledge the role of its opposite.

The creativity of chance

Many of the greatest inventions were the product of accident.

Researching a cure for cholera, Louis Pasteur injected a chicken with cholera bacteria, not realizing that the batch he was using had spoiled. The bird remained healthy not only then but also when later injected with active cholera bacteria. The chicken had become immune to the disease, an accident that led the French savant eventually to produce a vaccine!

When an Arabic merchant—legend has it—was traveling with some milk kept in a pouch made of sheep's stomach, the heat from the sun activated the tissue's enzymes and turned the milk into the solid curd that would eventually come to be known as cheese. (This was a very early incident; the earliest record of cheese dates back to 3500 BC.)

And what about the absentminded monk who unwittingly created Champagne?

When . . .

But I'll pause there. Examples of such serendipity run back to the origin of man and are endless. So when I salute a great invention, it would be unwise of me not to remember that it may have come from both chance and planning. (Which is not to say that all inventions, accidental or not, are great. The history of innovation is strewn with **useless inventions**. Oh, don't get me started on that!)

There's an essential balance between organizing and extemporizing. As my talented friend the choreographer Twyla Tharp writes: "Too much planning implies you've got it all under control. That's boring, unrealistic, and dangerous."*

Right on!

And yet, in my contradictory world, one thing is certain: the plan must be infallible! I'll explain how and why that is so.

Quest for perfection

One day, I was in the midst of lecturing on the pursuit of perfection when suddenly I switched to an improvised, mimed illustration of how I conceive of it.

I walked slowly from one side of the stage all the way to the other, until I collided (gently) with the proscenium wall.

I thought I had extracted the essence of my philosophy on the matter: it hurts to arrive at your destination, because there is nowhere further to go. The journey to perfection, my little demonstration meant to show, proved somewhat imperfect simply because it led to an end.

How naive I was to fall prey to such simplistic exposition!

I should have gone to the blackboard, drawn a snake coiled around a cylinder, and explained: "The cylinder is ice, is perfection. The snake, the seeker, wraps itself around it and stores the cold, soaks up perfection. The ice melts. The snake becomes ice, becomes perfection. In this journey, it is the path that will transform me, not the arrival."

*Twyla Tharp, *The Creative Habit* (New York: Simon & Schuster, 2003).

And along that path to perfection, I am sure to encounter detours. Detours that want to steal me away from my journey.

I think of these detours as *details that have not yet been awakened*. It is for the artist to decide which detours to take, which details to wake up, and which are better left asleep. Therefore, the path to perfection must be trod carefully and with great wisdom. You are drawing the map as you inch along. The Spanish poet Antonio Machado said it beautifully: *"Caminante, no hay camino."* (My translation: For the real traveler there is no path.)

Most detours—most details—should be welcomed as enriching the path. But not all. For example, a friend of mine cannot cook dinner without interrupting herself every minute to wipe clean—excruciatingly clean—her white Formica counter. This is not perfection, it is insanity.

By way of counterexample—and by way of inspiration—it took the greatest juggler in the world countless years of constant practice and rehearsal to hone to perfection his eight-minute juggling act. I would refer to these years as Francis Brunn's path toward perfection, and the fascinating balance of opposites he achieved (between sophistication and simplicity) as the inspiring *detail-detour* he encountered (and mastered) in his path.

Francis displayed a unique blend of simple moves (he balanced a soccer ball on his forehead) with sophisticated detail (he held the ball perfectly still for a few seconds); and sophisticated moves (he continuously threw six hoops in the air in an asymmetrical shower) with a simple detail (he used white hoops, so that they traced in the air a single hypnotic trail).

Come with me on one last detour, a path-to-perfection made of stone.

Today, as I have done a thousand times before, I sneak into the spiral staircase that drills up through the thick granite wall of the nave of the Cathedral of St. John the Divine (*my* cathedral), to reach the always deserted Triforium Gallery. There my life as Artist-in-Residence suspends between the *Done* (archives of past crimes) and the *To Do* (plans and models for future endeavors).

But on this particular evening, for the first time ever, I do not turn on the lights at the bottom of the stairs. I penetrate the pitch-black vertical passage with the excitement of a novice being initiated into a secret society and—is it to thicken the already total darkness?—childishly I close my eyes.

I start to climb.

Without difficulty my feet recognize the blunt stone treads; I am barely off the ground when already I feel surrounded! The cool inner wall, which I caress with one hand to secure my way, surrounds me with the power of the Great Wall of China.

Today's ascent illustrates my search for perfection; which is doubly fitting, because for me this stairway *is* perfection.

Drawn up in 1890 by the architects Heins and LaFarge, it is of impeccable design. Its superbly identical sixty-two steps smoothly wind around a central solid core of stone to the Triforium Gallery at a height of ninety-eight feet. In 1920, it was perfectly built from flawless limestone ashlars that came from the state of Indiana.

As I progress, each step offers an ephemeral pause in the present. The steps behind represent the past, the steps ahead the future. I surrender, one step at a time, to the relentless spiral of that enormous Archimedean screw which sucks me into another dimension.

Lost in obscurity, soon I no longer know if I am still climbing counterclockwise or if the masonry cylinder has suddenly shifted to a clockwise mode. If so, am I descending? The next moment I swear I'm progressing through a horizontal tunnel carpeted with steps.

No, perfection is not unreachable.

And yes, the path to perfection can be alarming.

Nevertheless, the quest for perfection must become the motor driving the artist.

Do not allow critics to make you think you're so good it's impossible for you to become better! Do not content yourself with merely reaching high standards to satisfy your ego. True artists enrich their art, not themselves.

Be the *Artist-in-Residence* (the *AIR*) of the *Cathedral of Your Dreams*. Store inside you the marvels you collect through your own climbing!

Get your act together

I don't mean "Get your act together!" I mean, get your act together, assemble an ensemble.

The plot thickens when the performing artist brings practice to the state of readiness that transports the work into the elements of what will be its final form.

Fueled by the pursuit of perfection—and reaping the bounty of detail the plan has awakened—I rush ahead to glue parts together.

By virtue of creative eagerness, a rough ensemble has no choice but to emerge.

It is akin to what I was told to do in preparation for my first oil painting when I was ten years old: Trace the outline of shapes with a thin stick of charcoal, and with a soft one indicate the dark and light tones (the values) that will later be replaced by the paint's color and density. On the wire, I put together a rather naive collage of well-executed movements, to which I add pieces of music. When I sense the little program (a *routine*, in show-business lingo) has the promise of a theatrical presentation (an *act*), I stretch it or compact it until its timing satisfies the member of the audience I become for a moment.

Soon I notice under my feet the birth of a new creation! But it will slip through my toes if I do not quickly knead it into the desired final shape. And it will refuse to bloom if I treat it simply as a routine exercise, instead of feeling it as an adventure. Now the new creation needs to acquire certain manners and education before I deem it worthy to be introduced to the out-side world!

I hurriedly add two new instruments to my orchestra: the "what is missing" and the "polish and hone" voices. They bring forth what frames a fine per-formance: costume, lights, full musical program, set design, special effects, stage direction . . .

Now that *the act* is born, I am ready to immerse myself in an entirely differ-ent creative effort than practicing; I must rehearse.

The rehearsal process

"These days I cannot learn anything new because I'm busy perfecting my three-ball reverse-cascade." As I was teaching myself to juggle at fourteen, this line from a 1947 juggling manual got me to imagine the juggler repeating the same move a thousand times, leaving no time for anything else! To this day that sentence remains one of my most powerful inspirations.

In 1971, in a half-empty Parisian parking lot, I spent hours with an accomplice perfecting the throw-and-catch of a rubber ball that would carry a fishing line from one tower of Notre Dame to the other, allowing the walk-cable to be pulled across and rigged for my illegal walk. (We only shattered one windshield.)

A few months before that, I had decided to briefly impose my aerial presence under the magnificent cupola of the Grand Palais (my very first walk without permission, which created a minor scandal). Dvořák's Sonatina for Violin and Piano in G major, Opus 100, spitting out of a cheap tape recorder was the musical frame I devised for the single high-wire crossing. Once I chose which movement to play, I rehearsed the walk on the floor of an abandoned warehouse so my steps would be in accord with the music, Antonín's last note coinciding with my arrival step.

To my criminal mind, rehearsing is paramount, no matter the form the crime takes.

When working on the composition of a chapter I am writing, first I review the group of relevant topics I've selected, deciding which to keep and which to discard. Then I try several ways to develop my ideas. To illustrate them I assign examples, I choose stories. I toy with different combinations until I come up with a valid ensemble that expresses what was in my mind.

This is very much like practice.

But when I actually write the chapter, I enter a process that is very much like rehearsal.

I go over each portion of the ensemble, to edit and polish its content. I inspect each group of words with the scrutiny of a reviewer. I challenge, I question: "Why is this there?" I repeatedly check over the flight formation of my paragraphs: what makes them interdependent in spirit, what links them together, how valid are the connections?

Then, one page at a time, I ensure that the fluidity of the text satisfies me.

Next, I read several pages carefully, on the lookout for intellectual holes or textual deformities. At the end, I go through the entire text three times: first to clean up any remaining incidents; second to receive the impact of the piece as a whole; and last to try to forget I'm the author and discover the chapter as if I were a reader new to the work.

But the process of rehearsal is not always so simple, especially when it's a complex performance piece that's being developed.

My struggle with results during rehearsal

Where should I focus my attention? On the technical collage of actions? On the best interpretation each individual segment deserves? On the feeling of fluidity—the *continuity*—a performer should experience throughout a finished piece? Or on my performing, my *presence*? Or on the delicate harmony that should frame the presentation as a whole?

Everywhere!

That's why the multifaceted task of rehearsing is extremely demanding.

When I work on a performance piece, I absorb the complexity of the act until it becomes second nature: I control the unfolding of the routine; lose myself in its artistic style; keep an eye on every detail (cues need to be given to signal changes in light and music); I mature my sense of timing and space, I imagine the audience's reactions, and all the while I try to lose myself inside the performance *and* become the critic who collects notes that will be used at the next rehearsal to improve the show!

I'll keep finding flaws, and I'll keep correcting them.

Sometimes a rehearsal will go disastrously awry. Because the elements I brought to the work were not ripe yet, or because circumstances decided to plot a fiasco—whatever the reason, there is a lot to profit from a "lost rehearsal": I see more clearly what is faulty or missing and I feel my quest for perfection is rekindling.

Not long before my WTC escapade, I tried to hold a rigging rehearsal. I was driven with a ton of equipment to an inclined, swampy piece of land surrounded by bushes near New Paltz, New York—not at all the dry, flat land with trees my three "helpers" (met by chance at the eleventh hour) had promised to provide!

Absentminded detours on the part of my driver—and maybe the inhalation of some substance I never tried—delayed our arrival until it was much too late for me to instruct my crew in the intricacies of a high-wire installation having unusual anchor points and custom-made guy-lines called *cavalettis*.

In the face of rapidly approaching darkness (we had no source of light but the moon), I had to gallop through the complex technical assembly by myself, performing every part in the entire "rigging play" while my "actors" merely watched.

And then it started to rain.

The operation did not help my so-called helpers, but it did help me. It tightened the vise of my determination to the point of insanity. It reminded me that I would one day install that wire between the two towers, come hail or come hell, even if I had to do it, as on that evening, all on my own; and even if I had, for good measure, the entire world against me.

Even if you are not a performer, even if you don't have an act, do not think that you have nothing to rehearse!

The art of living makes a performing artist out of you.

Rehearse your next day before it awakens you.

Rehearse your dream before it evaporates.

Rehearse with pride and joy, and lose yourself in the pleasure of performing your daily life!

But . . . keep on the lookout for those creeping waves of inattention and diminishing energy that create an ever-growing distance between you and your goal.

When they arise—and they will—I have an antidote. It is made of three ingredients, which may be taken in unequal doses at any time, not necessarily in the following order:

- Intuition

- Improvisation

- Observation

Intuition

I almost wish to impose a minute of silence in homage to this most important topic in my creative world. Actually, it is such a *wide-and-wild* notion that it should not even be presented as a "topic" but rather explored as a continent.

Intuition is the incommensurable force that can shape and transport mountains in a matter of seconds. Its effectiveness resides in the fact that it is rooted deep within your own personality, thus it *always* agrees with you—and because it follows your natural inclination, it is effortless to acquire and operate.

There are rules, there is common sense, there is wisdom, there is professional know-how, and there are many other ways to bring a project to fruition or solve a problem . . . and then there is intuition. It offers a rainbow of joyful permutations, each sure to win your heart (and, in my opinion, to save the day).

If I don't always yield to what my intuition proposes, at least I make a point of contemplating what it has in store for me *before* I decide to engage a different motor of creation. (Why is this simple art not taught in our schools? Because it gives individuals too much intellectual power?)

Does intuition save lives? Oh, yes.

In my four decades as a New Yorker, I have often greeted the foreign visitors I've guided through my beloved adopted metropolis with disdain for their clichéd fear of the city. "I've never been mugged!" I declare, explaining that this has nothing to do with my being lucky.

When I plan to venture into a dicey neighborhood, I make a point of wearing battered clothes rather than my Parisian three-piece suit. Because I read body language, I can size up from a distance a gang-looking group of people, and decide to cross the street a block ahead rather than pass them on a sidewalk they might "own." And if someone accosts me in Times Square, brandishing a map and with just a little too much zeal to be, in my opinion, a genuine tourist, I play it safe and fake being Russian (understanding not a word of English), which sends the suspected impostor to find a victim elsewhere in the crowd . . .

A dark September evening in Sheridan Square, I am street-juggling in my circle surrounded by people from New York and all over the world when I catch a glimpse of a kid in the front row on the far side of the circle. As I approach him, I palm my magic coin and then reach behind his ear to produce a silver surprise. Surprise it is! My spectator is not a child but a midget (I am told the appropriate term is "little man"). I guess my glimpse wasn't my best glimpse.

With no time to formulate how to erase the confusion or beg for forgiveness, I abandon myself to the moment and let my intuition lead.

I show the coin to the entire audience in an elegant circular gesture a torero would envy, then I lock it into my fist. I bring my fist in front of the little man's mouth and mime silently: *Blow on it!*

He does.

But not strongly enough to cause the coin to disappear.

So I mime again: *Blow . . . harder!* And after he does, I slowly unfold my fingers to reveal that thanks to him the coin has vanished.

With a smile of complicity, showing appreciation for his magic breath, I shake the man's hand. We celebrate with a burst of synchronized laughter.

Although intuition is capable of much force, I see it as a sensitive feather, and as such, I manipulate this virtue with utmost care (mostly when reason whispers that it is time to brush aside intuition or blend it with new influences). For intuition alone can't always single-handedly operate the machinery of creativity.

Improvisation

If intuition is the left hand of creativity, improvisation is the right—another essential means of guiding the imagination to produce tangible consequences.

Improvisation has been my credo for forty-five years of street-juggling all over the world (and I'm not about to give it up!). Being a juggler of only average talent, I actually use juggling as an excuse to occupy my circle of chalk and gather a crowd with whom I can then play silently, improvising in a comic way.

Riding my unicycle, I carry an old leather bag (used to deliver mail in Paris, circa 1900). It contains the props I need for the show and some that I use from time to time when I feel like it, but I also throw in the bag several odd objects found here and there by chance that I intend to use by chance.

For instance, I have a fake piece of delicious-looking sushi made out of colored rubber (stolen in Prague from the window of one of those cheap restaurants that cater to lazy tourists who do not want to read menus). I have a tiny three-minute hourglass (the type you use to time the boiling of an egg). I have a plastic black spider (enormous for my arachnophobic taste, but nevertheless small enough to lodge inside my hand) that I can wind and let wend on the sidewalk until it needs rewinding. And I have a sheriff's star found in a dime store to which I have added a bit of Velcro so I can stick it to anyone's coat at any moment—don't ask me why.

I let these objects slumber inside my mailbag until one day, in the midst of a performance, one of them calls on me to improvise a duo on the spot!

If you ask me, "What kind of improvised scene would you do with such props?" I would instantly come up with one answer. For example:

• I notice a young lady in the front row finishing her sandwich so I swiftly pick a large leaf from the nearest tree, run to my bag and pick up the sushi portion, which I place on the leaf with a pair of chopsticks (that I also always carry in my bag), and offer it to her as an addition to her meal.

• I pass the hat at the conclusion of my show and stand in front of an old man who takes his time looking for change in all his pockets; I dive into the bag, grab the hourglass, reverse it and plant it at the man's feet, with a smile that says: "Sure, take your time, you have three minutes!"

• I interrupt my three-ball routine because I see from the corner of my eye a hefty cockroach crossing the chalk line and invading my theatrical territory (yes, I can juggle and observe at the same time—my hands and the balls being old accomplices, they do not require my visual supervision at all times). To ward off the trespasser, I simply wind up the spider and send her into the path of the visiting insect, watching "him" U-turn in terror.

• As for the sheriff's badge, I hear in the crowd the static of a walkie-talkie growing near until I see a uniformed security guard struggling his way into the front row: I instantly retrieve the silver star, slap it on my black turtleneck and, imitating John Wayne's gait, approach the man. I point disapprovingly at the tips of his shoes trespassing in my circle. He quickly backs up an inch, for which I shake his hand with a smirk of complicity—after all, we belong to the same trade: law enforcement!

Now, having revealed some of the myriad ways my street character would play with such props, I would be cheating if I used them precisely that way during upcoming circles (that's how I refer to my continuous performances in the park), because to improvise is to surprise yourself.

In the memory of my life lie countless examples of situations when my instinct to perform without preparation—to improvise against all rules or against all odds—saved the day.

Secretly scouting the basement of the Twin Towers during my spy work, I noticed a policeman looking at me from behind (he just came out of a tiny police station I did not know existed). There was no way I could pull out my measuring tape and check the height of the loading dock (my mission for the day)—and no way I would ever come back scouting this area now that I knew there was a police station there! Without thinking, I quickly rubbed my chest against the dirty edge of the high platform and calmly walked away, carrying indelibly on my white T-shirt the line for the exact measurement I needed.

Maybe it is because I am in the habit of preparing so thoroughly that when I dismount the galloping horse of expectations, my improvisations rarely fail.

If to improvise is to welcome the unknown, I must dress accordingly! After shedding my doubts and expectations, I put on my innocence and openness and slip honesty and generosity on top. I keep those habits (pun intended) throughout the entire creative process.

Beware: as its name implies, improvisation does not announce itself. It lands anywhere along the creative process, during rehearsal or in performance— and once gone, it doesn't leave you a business card.

One day I'll confess that I cheat.

I don't *improvise*, I *run in the direction dictated by my intuition*. So if I always do that, I'm not improvising, am I? But my intuition seldom travels unidirectionally, so therefore, I *do* improvise (and I don't cheat)!

A great producer must be a great improviser. My friend James Signorelli proves it, day in, day out. I've seen him improvise to solve problems on a movie set, then improvise inside of his own improvisation to solve more problems—all the while making people smile with his relentless good humor.

The art of improvisation is for me the art of diving from an elevated spring-board. I appreciate the speed of the takeoff; I revel in the sudden abandon of intellectual safety; I salute the point of no return. And I am always concerned with the uncertainty of the result—at times I don't even have time to check if the swimming pool is filled with water or to remember that I do not know how to swim.

Observation

In 1240, the Englishman Sir Roger Bacon offered profound advice to anyone with the desire to learn: "Contemplate the world!"

It is all here for us to take!

Nature is our first master waiting to be drawn from. Then come others, from the human family. Each has something to offer us.

To learn: study and assimilate, study and imitate.

All you have to do is look.

To see is not enough.

Observe, I say—and contemplate.

Observation is one of my master words and another principal source of my creativity.

I make a point of observing. But not only with my sense of sight.

When I want to teach myself a new language, I start by closely "observing" the nature of its music. I listen to recordings and repeat them endlessly—even if I don't yet understand every word—focusing on rhythm and tone as much as on accent.

But as I look thoughtfully, as I observe the world around me, I also *self-observe*. Keen inspection works in both directions; it allows me to discover the unusual that hides inside me as well as outside.

For example, in museums I hunt for anomalies in paintings: a person's hand with four or six fingers (nature's work or the artist's mischief?); a shadow that stretches in the wrong direction; a banner that floats *toward* the wind . . .

Years ago I started an iconographic collection of what I call "wrong lays": drawings, paintings, sculptures that depict an impossible rope construction—when you twist strands to form a rope, the final product shows a left or a right twist (the lay), but never both! Today my album is filled with the work of "guilty" artists, among them Leonardo da Vinci. (If you do not believe me, follow with your eyes the single rope that dresses his giant crossbow: it starts with left lay and ends with right lay!)

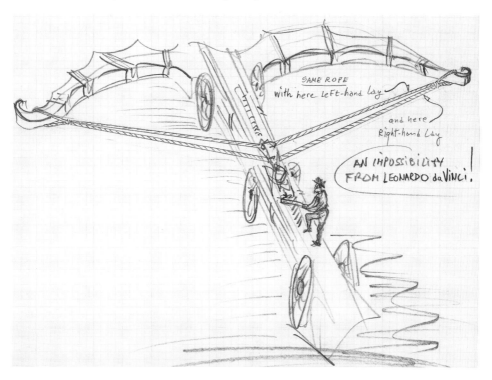

I have been caught adding shadows to magazine illustrations that did not have any. I enjoy the result: a scene suddenly wakes up and shapes up, newly grounded in reality.

Even when I dedicate my eyes to the action of reading, I observe!

I open a book and already at the tip of my fingers comes a pencil set on automatic pilot. It corrects typos almost without my noticing (and it also jots in the margin my reactions to the book's content!).

Among the infinite advantages of cultivating the *art of observation* is the natural increase in detours-details (a misdirection of sorts) that present themselves when I order my senses to switch on their searchlights.

Remain alert! Observe relentlessly! I silently remind myself every minute as I practice or rehearse. If I don't, I'll end up slouching, mentally and physically. The mind keeps the body on the tightrope of harmony, while an aligned body keeps the mind sharp and active.

Keeping your observation antennas active opens you to another wonder: the language of the human body.

Body language

Body language is universal.

In a park in Chinatown, from a distance, I followed an old man with my eyes for a long time.

He was dragging his feet around and around the park, as if remembering a time when he was able to jog. His body seemed to follow his steps with a slight delay. His face gave hints of struggle and pain. His stiff, skinny frame tried to readjust the balance disturbed by each new step. When he stopped to greet a friend, he held on to the other man's sleeve, as if leaning for rest instead of solely emphasizing something being said. But when he waved good-bye, he was unable to turn his torso or even his neck to see his friend depart; in order to look over his shoulder he had to make a complete body rotation!

Watching him, I began to feel his rustiness in *my* body. Then, behind some bushes, as an experiment the mime in me imitated what I had observed and . . . I became an old man!

You see (pun intended), when I observe, I imitate.

When I imitate, I internalize the observation. I store it where I can feed on it. Then I am capable of becoming what I have observed, because what my body assimilates through observation imprints my soul.

That's how I learn. That's how I create.

But this I did not invent.

This is how human civilization works.

This is what rules the animal kingdom.

Babies learn by imitating adults.

Predators size up prey.

A would-be mate gauges a potential partner's attraction.

Animal or human, a frail, isolated being senses if the approach of a strong pack means social conviviality or deadly threat.

How do we observe others?

The eyes, the eyes . . . yes, the eyes, of course the eyes!

It is first the eyes that permit us to evaluate—or so we trust—a human being at a glance.

And yet, a maître d'hôtel or casino director might appraise clients' wealth with a discreet glance at their shoes, and will greet guests with a wide smile that if immediately returned will allow a fugacious dental inspection! But as revealing as the bodily trappings we deliberately adopt are, it is the unconscious language our bodies speak that expresses loudly what we may wish to keep silent: the movements that animate our limbs, the muscular contractions we add to our faces, the tone of voice we use, the spatial relation we adopt (to humans and objects). They have adapted to our moods and glued to our personality.

Interpreting body language is a complex science, and there are countless books on the subject. Yet anyone with a keen sense of observation and a minor dose of common sense can read it.

If your host greets you at the threshold with the warm welcome "My house is your house!" but has her arms and ankles crossed, you can be sure she wishes you would not come in!

If the boss calls you in for an "open discussion," then leans back in his plush chair, extends both arms and lays his hands flat on the desk, fingers apart, he's reminding you of his power while holding on (with both hands) to his "empire"—he won't be likely to share anything with you. And, if you could see through the desk his feet furiously wagging, you would know he wants to use them as soon as possible—that is, to get the hell out of here and abandon you!

In life, everyone could, everyone should, exercise their talent for reading body language—and not only artists and performers.

Imagine the architect sketching a fireplace. How high? How wide? She should take into consideration the positions the human body will take. To feed the logs to the fire, will you have to kneel, crouch or bend? To relax by the flames, will you lie down on a carpet or pull up an armchair?

Imagine the writer so focused on the psychological traits of his protagonist that he neglects to add flesh. You'd have a tale of bodiless phantoms!

Mastering body language allows you to speak it as well as interpret it. It allows you to direct—or misdirect—the attention of your audience, even when you haven't invited them.

Early in the morning of the WTC adventure, after rigging all night, Jean-François and I were feverishly finishing tightening the cavaletti lines, knowing that the construction crew would be arriving at any minute.

Suddenly, out of nowhere, a well-dressed visitor appeared. Instantly, I adopted the body language of a typical construction worker. I lifted my helmet to scratch my forehead; I reached for my tools with slow, controlled hand motions. I continued working, but with apparent nonchalance and a touch of laziness, as if this were just my job and it was a tad early for me to show any zeal. My observant friend had the intuition to imitate my behavior. The man looked at the cable stretched between the towers. He ran his eyes along each cavaletti. He noticed the balancing-pole tied to the corner of the roof. But he only watched us for a minute and, apparently satisfied that we were just regular workers, he left.

Magicians, ventriloquists and pickpockets know the value of the science (for me, the art) of *misdirection*. They pitch their body language to hide certain actions that, if visible, would instantly compromise their performance.

I honed my skills as a pickpocket by following for days the stage act of the grand master Borra while he was on tour. No matter how often I witnessed his performance, my eyes could never quite catch him red-handed for long.

Borra always started his inimitable pickpocket act with a brief magic performance with lit cigarettes. He'd lean forward, lit cigarette in hand, in order to blow a ring of smoke through another ring already floating in midair.

Everyone was observing with intense concentration this extraordinary ethereal penetration of the rings, including me—even though I knew (but could never see!) that in the act of leaning forward, the master's other hand was openly stealing another lit cigarette from a *charger* (holding-device) hidden in the lining of his tuxedo! The *load* (in magician's parlance), which took a fraction of a second, was genius because it was not hidden from view and yet it remained invisible to all. Borra was then able to vanish the cigarette he was holding (by dropping it invisibly in his *topit*—a large pocket inside his jacket) and, after showing that hand to be empty, made the audience believe he was plucking from the air with the other hand a freshly lit cigarette (the one he got from the charger).

Here again, I would say, in *ordinary life* everyone could, everyone should, exercise their creative right to misdirect—and not only magicians, pickpockets, ventriloquists and their close cousin, the con artist!

Imagine the motion-picture director—Hitchcock comes to mind instantly— who deliberately emphasizes a detail in a scene, solely to pull your thoughts in the opposite direction of what is actually going to happen. *Misdirection of suspicion!*

What the plan exhales

Enough misdirection! Let's get back to the plan. We would be impoverished if, as the plot thickens, we left the master plan behind.

Instead, we must revisit it constantly, because it will seal our every move to-gether, from here until the coup.

To plan becomes for me now to sow and harvest in a single action. And it warrants each time another furtive intrusion into my *Cathedral of Creativity*—to load in new crates of thoughts, to retrieve missing bits, or simply to read what the geography of the place has in store for me that day.

Thanks to intuition, improvisation and observation, I update my plan con-stantly. But more importantly, it updates me. I inhale what the plan exhales.

Constantly revisiting the plan prepares the artist mentally and physically for the coup ahead. It acts as an intellectual rehearsal: every step of the action gets revisited. It's a bit like the way a knot-expert, through constant practice, transmits to his fingers the dynamics of specific hitches and bends, ensuring that the knots will tie "automatically" in an emergency situation—ensuring his survival.

The evening of the WTC coup, my "dress rehearsal" inside a Chelsea sublet was pure and simple.

I stood up and let my memory recite aloud several times in a row the entire plan of action—drafted and redrafted over the previous six and a half years (and, of course, written and rewritten over the final two and a half days).

I kept talking until the coup and its various acts and scenes dissolved into a liquid mass that infiltrated my veins—until the air I breathed was the plan itself. Until I became the plan (in the same way, at the beginning of this book, in toying with a blank page I became the page).

True friends, false friends, whoever was in the room, witnessed that moment silently and silently laughed at my madness.

My advice to you forty years later: let them laugh.

Thank you for trekking with me.

The land we finished exploring was vast and diverse.

Through planning and chance we encountered a multitude of wildlife, details and perfection. We listened to the songs of the landscape: they were of hope and strength, of expectations and achievements.

Now they may send us upward, downward, running chaotically clockwise, counterclockwise, and—wise, unwise—they may wrap our senses in the kind of screaming darkness that enveloped my blind ascent inside the cathedral's spiral staircase.

Let's follow the voices, shrieking or whispering, that lead us to the edge of an abyss. We now stand in the position of the human silhouette in Caspar David Friedrich's painting *The Wanderer Above the Sea of Clouds*: alone and contemplating brightness from a place where everything is possible, from too high above.

Is there such a thing as *too high*?

((((((((useless inventions))))))))

Not all creativity is born equal.

Some inventors are blessed with vision, some (consciously or not) wear blinders.

Perhaps it's the desire to discover, to come up with something new—to be celebrated, to force-feed the ego—that hurls sometimes the impetuous creator in the wrong direction. Or perhaps sometimes it's the effect of too much feverish research in isolation that results in the invention of the unnecessary, the absurd, or, worse, the contra-creative.

Let's investigate the use and abuse of creativity!

When is something worth pursuing?

I think when the outcome advances the efforts of humanity.

Look at the carpenter's saw, for instance.

Thousands of years of woodworking have brought this hand tool to a state of perfect design and capability.

The handle marries the craftsman's hand; the hollow blade (it has been made thinner at the top than at the kerf, where the teeth are) reduces friction during the cutting action; the teeth have been shaped into a series of tiny blades for crosscutting or tiny chisels for ripping (sawing along the wood's grain), to bite the wood in the most effective, effortless way.

If you take any item used every day by everyone almost forever—let's say a toothbrush—and study it, dissect it, you might at best be able to come up with a slight modification that makes it a tiny bit more efficient. You are unlikely to be able to improve it significantly, because it doesn't need improvement.

But . . . when people use their creative talents to solve problems that don't exist, or toil intensely to redesign a tool that needs no amelioration, they come up with useless inventions.

For instance, does a peppercorn mill need a motor to replace the simple action of the human wrist? And if a motor must be added to the mill, does it need more than one speed? And should this new model have an embedded light? Of course, during a candlelit dinner date you don't want pepper to fall in the wrong place, do you? And while we're at it, why not add a compass, in case you get lost in a very large kitchen? "Sure" will be the answer of the collector of gadgets who expects his wristwatch to indicate, along with time, his longitude and latitude as well as which chess move he should make if he plays the Closed Ruy Lopez.

(((((((((((((((•)))))))))))))))

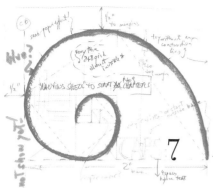

7 | A MURDER OF PROBLEMS

A good tap dancer does not look at his feet.

And here we were, dancing our achievements away, forgetting to look up.

Notice the gathering of dark clouds above our heads.

A storm is near. No, a devastating hurricane. Or is it the end of the world?

Let's talk about problems.

As I am busy feeding creative concepts to hungry ideas, problems invariably crawl in.

But long ago I found ways to solve them.

For one thing, they always trigger more than one solution—I can prove it!—so my friendship with problems comes from the pleasure to choose.

Ah . . . but how to fish for solutions?

Here is my secret: a problem does nothing all day (and all night) but whisper its solution—just listen!

To each problem its province

If it's a problem of fire, fire might very well be the answer.

Around campfires I delight in reenacting the story of an explorer in Africa, caught in a rapidly advancing fire on the savanna. The lifesaving solution to this desperate situation is to dig quickly—with a little shovel, the heel of your boot or your hands—a circular (roughly thirty feet in diameter) shallow trench to create a narrow, grassless boundary between the grass land soon to be engulfed by fire and the grass disc on which you stand. Now, step out of the circle and swiftly set fire to the grass inside. As soon as the fire dies, jump back in and lay flat, facedown. Keep breathing! You will suffer no more than minor burns. When the fire's front line arrives at the edge of the circle, the flames will stop because inside the circle there is no longer any dry grass for the fire to feed upon. Fire fights fire.

If there is a liquid involved in the problem at hand, most likely the problem can be solved by researching fluid properties. Think water, think air—in physics classes we were taught they behave very much alike.

Sometimes in my lectures I ask a volunteer to come onstage and drop a few playing cards one after the other into a large pan. I position the person's hand two feet above the center of the pan. Invariably the cards miss their target.

That's because the most natural way to hold a card before dropping it is to pinch one of its corners between the thumb and index finger, and let the card hang vertically. I confess I do not hesitate to mime this pinch to my "victim" to ensure this result: when freed, the little piece of shiny Bristol is caught by "liquid air" that makes it free-fall in a spiral, like a dead leaf—and miss the target.

The secret—and I go on demonstrating—is to hold the card perfectly horizontal above the pan by all four corners before opening your fingers suddenly, all at once. The little pasteboard is met on all sides by regular, symmetrical streams of air, ensuring its flat, regular descent: it hits the pan dead center!

NO!

Yes!

Students! I urge you to stop rummaging through the thick books-of-solutions forced on you by school administrators. Decipher instead the thoughts most problems write in thin air; follow with your eyes their subtle glances and feel their caresses.

Sometimes they write more than one solution. Then how do I know which is best? Ah, mirror, mirror on the wall, 'tis the most simple of them all!

Without quoting statistics—a language I despise—I am confident in declaring: the simplest solution is always the best. As Einstein remarked, "Everything should be made as simple as possible, not simpler."

And what if I face more than one simple solution?

Simple! Embrace the good-looking one, the sexy one; the one that pleases you, that brings a smile to your face—the one that is aesthetic, that shines with grace, transparency, balance or poetry.

For me, the best problem-solving team is:

Simplicity & Elegance.

Step back with me some four thousand years and try your hand at using the carpenter's vise depicted in bas-relief on the wall of an Egyptian tomb. Its principal elements: a sturdy supporting surface, a piece of rope, a human foot. Lay on the support the wooden piece you want to carve, throw an endless loop of cord* over the work, place one foot in

*To transform a twenty-four-inch length of rope into a strop (an endless loop), use the Double Sheet Bend as taught by the author in his book *Why Knot?* (New York: Abrams, 2013).

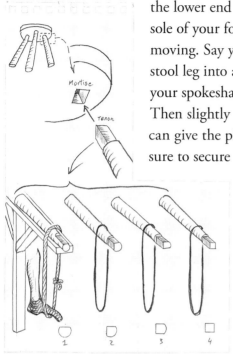

the lower end of the loop and apply pressure with the sole of your foot to prevent the wooden piece from moving. Say you are shaping the end of a cylindrical stool leg into a square tenon to fit a square mortise. Run your spokeshave to make the first flat face of the square. Then slightly release the pressure of your foot so you can give the piece a quarter of a turn; reapply the pressure to secure the piece again, and keep shaving. Repeat three times.

The jackals of negativity

"In every art there is a diabolical principle which acts against it and tries to demolish it," wrote the celebrated French moviemaker Robert Bresson.[*]

Fact: I am crushed by the weight of my larger-than-life goal.

Fact: My deadline is unattainable.

Fact: I'm using the wrong tools.

Fact: I lack the means of keeping my focus.

Fact: I can't do it alone, I need help.

The above exemplifies the sort of fabrications we are inclined to believe after a mixture of physical and intellectual fatigue invades our efforts.

*Robert Bresson, *Notes on the Cinematographer*, trans. Jonathan Griffin (Copenhagen: Green Integer, 1997).

In fact, they are not facts at all.

Nonetheless, these *excuses* transform into three-dimensional hazards, which in turn attract a murder of obstacles—"murder" as in a murder of crows—imaginary or Hitchcockianly real.

I know, because all of the above happen to me when I run too hard, too fast, too far, for too long—all of which I do on a regular basis. My overenthusiasm creates obstacles both imaginary and tangible, which in turn I have to overcome.

A "real" obstacle confronted me toward the end of my WTC adventure. Because I spent too much time refining a plan of attack and not enough investigating office policies inside the towers, I discovered very late in the game a sudden change in security: employees were now being required to carry a photo ID in the towers at all times.

My project came to a halt while I spent days rethinking, reorganizing and eventually forging the necessary documents.

In moments like these, when certainty dissolves without warning, what do I do?

At first, I have the longing to slow down—and that disturbs me. Then my energy (energy I had trusted to be limitless) reaches its exhaustion point—and that enrages me.

A short-circuit that will destroy all my work and sever my cord-of-desire is about to happen. I feel it coming, I notice the black clouds above my head, I worry.

Then, without warning (What would I do if I received warnings? Collect them? Make a list?), obstacles of all sorts litter my field like land mines. I grow scared.

Yet I refuse to yield to panic. (Where would that lead me? In circles? To a savanna on fire?) Instead, I come up with desperate questions—the wrong ones, of course.

I ask myself:

"Why did I miss . . . ?"

"Why am I unable to . . . ?"

"What is the right reaction to feeling surrounded by . . . ?"

"Am I surrounded by . . . ?"

"What should I do when . . . ?"

And on and on.

There is a short *Book of Questions* buried in the richness of Celtic mythology. It offers profound entries such as "What is the worst you've seen?" and "How do you distinguish a woman?"

But my questions are far from profound. Plus, I have no time to answer them. And how useful is it for me to try, when I should be busy clearing my path of all obstacles?

There is an art to questioning as well as an essential creative need: it creates openings, it provides connections.

When I enter a house that has all the windows and doors closed, I have the secret longing to open them wide so that the outside air with its outside influences can penetrate and rejuvenate those who are locked inside!

One day I'll come up with my own *Book of Questions*, directed at readers of all ages, but without the answers.

- Why do we have the reflex to crumple pieces of paper before we throw them in the wastebasket? They take up more space that way!

- Why does a tea bag twirl when you pull it out of the cup after steeping? And why almost always in a counterclockwise direction? In Australia, would it twirl clockwise?

- Why does almost every ad agency in the world set the time on a watch at 10:10 before photographing it?

- Where does the decision to package a dozen eggs per carton come from—why not ten or nine, or thirteen?

- How did someone come up with this piece of advice I read in a cookbook: "Wet the blade of your knife with a little bit of white wine before you cut garlic"?

Enough!

The first discovery I made—triggered by arrogance, by stubbornness?—was not to turn away when I encountered a wall blocking my path.

Obviously, most of the time I lack the strength to topple the wall. So I inspect it for weaknesses that could work to my advantage. If none are found at first glance, I concentrate my inspection on minute areas that I examine like Sherlock Holmes . . . until under my magnifying glass I discover a minuscule fissure. There is always at least one; no wall (like no human) is perfect.

That's a start, I think.

Encouraged by that thought, I attack the fissure with a pick, a teaspoon, my nails, until it enlarges into a narrow crevasse wide enough for me to sneak through and continue my journey.

Mistakes of solid gold

Adversity, or even the mere suggestion of it, fogs our judgment. After the hardship, after the questions, after the struggle against obstacles, when our impaired judgment leaves us with the taste of disaster, something else seemingly falls from the sky: giant mistakes!

In my lectures, I mime sawing a piece of wood for a few seconds, then, as I continue to saw, I salute an imaginary friend passing by and—a short scream of pain startles my audience—I've just cut myself!

"You see," I tell them, "it is entirely my fault. First, I allowed myself to be distracted. Maybe I did not check the wood for knots that could make the blade jump or for spots of humidity that could cause it to get stuck. Maybe I did not inspect the saw for misaligned teeth. Maybe I had not sharpened it properly."

The enumeration of causes—which we like to disguise into excuses—is often quite long. But for me no excuse is ever valid.

However, in my life of trials and errors, mistakes have always been my most persuasive teachers and, naturally, the toughest.

Mistakes are my confidants. And in a secret way I cherish them!

Wouldn't it be a great idea to add a mistakes course to the curriculum of our schools? "Okay, Tuesday I want you all to make mistakes; we're going to learn from them. Don't cheat—no bringing in mistakes you've already made!"

Talented actors have in them the ability to *lean* on a mistake, to profit from it. If in the middle of a scene they suddenly forget a line, they do not abandon the action or cripple the dialogue; they stay in character and use the hesitation or the sudden silence to add substance to the situation. In fact, as long as it respects the spirit of the scene, an improvised recovery may actually enrich the play!

Avoid "tips" on how to avoid mistakes. They are usually brainless or brainwashing; they will mislead you, they will blindfold you.

For example, the carpenter's old adage "Measure twice, cut once" makes me angry. It is an invitation to not pay attention. It is an ode to intellectual laziness and a call to stop caring. It will rob you of your intelligence. Its fateful effects will multiply exponentially, invading the rest of your life. Think. Focus. Then, like me, measure once and cut once.

By the way, I keep one mistake in the middle of my living room! I look at it often, visitors compliment me on it, and it keeps offering its practical service faithfully.

It is a large, deep cigar-ashtray, carved out of a short piece of four-by-six hemlock. I confess, it came from the first beam I sawed to make my barn. Actually, from the very first cut. My impatience to start caused me to bore and chisel a perfect mortise on a long sill-piece—but unfortunately at the wrong spot!

By sawing off both sides and filing a little resting groove for my cigar, I transformed my mistake into an ashtray that I enjoy almost as much as I do my Cohiba Robusto cigars—always in moderation, of course. (I am trying to be politically correct here, but I suspect any reader of mine will know by now that *immoderation* was the word I really meant to use.)

Put your mistakes to good use, I say.

If you're a painter and you have just destroyed a canvas with a work you are ashamed of, don't throw it away and don't try to scrape off the oil paint with a spatula. Paint over it! But not over it to cover the first image, cover it with art and imagination! Let some of the earlier work surface here and there, using linseed oil and turpentine to force the original pigment to surface, creating surprising overlaps.

That's exactly what Picasso did with *Les Demoiselles d'Avignon*: instead of trashing a painting not to his liking he kept adding new work on top of the old one. And it shows!

Of course, you can play with mistakes.

raef

That's *fear* backward.

For *fear* is nothing but the mirror image of a contretemps. We should all develop the reflex of brushing it away, for fear that fear might temper our ardor—which it will. Fear is a springboard designed in reverse.

Look in the mirror of fear and focus beyond it. What appears in the background is your path, awaiting.

I'll add that fear of making mistakes makes you make more mistakes, which in turn invites mistakes to be made mistakenly!

The only fear I experience in the vicinity of an illegal high-wire walk is fear itself. I'm afraid to imagine that one day I'll have to give up the wire, as so many bullfighters have abandoned the arena, simply because I'm afraid of walking in the sky. Other than that, I'm too busy.

But on the ground, oh yes, I have "down to earth" fears.

What scares me?

Creatures with too many legs or no legs at all. Centipedes, snakes, a giant spider slowly stretching her eight hairy legs.

When I finally decide it is time to conquer that silly terror, I know damn well how to proceed.

I'll watch documentaries, I'll read science reports, I'll go to the zoo, I'll interview spider wranglers. I'll learn as much as I can about the monster—its food preferences, its mating and hunting habits, and, most important (my revenge on fear), what frightens the scary beast!

Then, like James Bond, I won't have any problem having a tarantula dance a tarantella on my forearm.

React to fright by burying your mind in knowledge, not your head in the sand; or print this: "Fear is the absence of knowledge; to know is to love." And pin up that poster in your dormitory!

"You're under arrest!"

At WTC, I got caught.

Months before my wire-walk, that is.

I had just returned to New York from Paris and had gone directly to the roof of the North Tower to check on the progress of the structural work.

As soon as I emerged on the concrete slab hovering 1,350 feet above Manhattan, a police officer jumped on me. He eventually copied my passport and threatened to have me sent back to Europe if I ever set foot in the towers again—"or if I even see you around this neighborhood!"

That sliced my dream in two like the saber stroke of a calm samurai. It triggered an extreme derailment (is there another kind?) of my creative process.

I tried to forget the Twin Towers, I even looked for new buildings in Manhattan to replace them, I focused on other pursuits . . . to no avail. Within two weeks my beloved towers were back solidly standing inside my head, and the dream had rekindled.

The impact is exactly the same when the police interrupt one of my street-juggling performances—where there is no life at stake, where the dream in question is simply for me to spend a couple of hours in a park entertaining passers-by. Uniforms suddenly invade the middle of my performance (never the end—how come?) and disturb the delicate construction of my improvisations. Strangely, I never could adjust to that cruel behavior, although I've been arrested more than five hundred times. Well, at least I've stopped counting!

Being betrayed, being caught. Two sides of a false coin, which for me are the same.

An arrow in the heart

What's the problem with a wire-walker being shot by an arrow in the heart? Oh, nothing—it's just that I can't let go of the balancing-pole to use both hands to pull out the arrow and keep walking!

A most painful *funambulesque* defeat happened in Switzerland several decades ago. Four days before the walk, my crew and I had finished passing a heavy steel cable high over fifteen roofs in the center of Lausanne and had secured both ends to solid anchors, following a month of rigging preparations.

True to high-wire traditions, we celebrated on the arrival roof with cold

Champagne in crystal flutes . . . when the bad news hit us: the local producer had not lived up to his responsibilities, and by failing to provide the necessary equipment, manpower and security, he was endangering the event and my life.

Kathy, as the executive producer representing my side of the project, and I were left with a simple choice: we could add the finishing touches to the rigging as best we could and present the high-wire crossing as announced for months on large posters throughout the city—and in doing so, seriously compromise the structural integrity of the departure and arrival buildings, potentially endangering the lives of thousands of spectators (and by having me walk on a shaky installation, framing my miserable existence with a giant question mark). Or we could cancel the event.

My choice was made even before the sentence containing the bad news had ended: "Let's go ahead, work harder, day and night, and make it all happen, although in the worst conditions possible—it won't be the first time."

Never in my life had I canceled an officially announced high-wire walk. I was not about to do it today.

Kathy took stock of the situation and saw a disaster in the making. "Let's refuse disaster," she said. "Cancel, and explain why."

During the excruciating hours leading to a final decision, disillusion and frustration made it hard for me to keep breathing. And after a press conference, at which I explained why I was forced to cancel, despair and rage nearly asphyxiated me. Only long after we had left behind the delinquent local organization, the disgruntled city officials and even our palace-like hotel (escaping like thieves although we were the victims) and crossed borders and time—really, only when I had begun work on my next walk in New York (above the concourse of Grand Central Terminal) did the deadly defeat I felt begin to diffuse—even though I understand today it was a life-affirming victory.

I can show you the scars left on my heart by other such arrow shots that pierce me in utter despair even today.

I could go on to invoke further examples of creative interruptions that slammed the handcuffs on my dreams.

But what good would come of it?

The complete derailment of any creative project beyond the control of the artist for me equals human death—a point of no return that cannot be fought.

Which leads me—and you, if you're still holding on for hope—into the very dark land of hopelessness.

Tunnels of hopelessness

You have been brought to death's door and now you're losing hope!

You're unsure.

You're invaded by doubts.

You're suffocating from worries.

You've heard a kid complain: "It's not fair . . . it always rains when I go outside to play!"

You are aware of the absurdity of taking such injustices personally . . . and yet you glance at the rain and you feel punished! Now it is a deluge—dogs and cats and tarantulas—and your visibility has been reduced to the length of a centipede.

So you slow down.

You stop.

And you look at the bolts of lightning that land around you, so close, so close, and you wonder . . . but you can't even pray. You're nearly dead because you've seen the *Impossible* stick out its nose!

When I review the path of my life and its incentives to stop walking, I think of my little Gypsy and listen to my friend Paco Ibañez singing José Agustín Goytisolo's poem "Palabras para Julia" (Words for Julia) set to music, with the participation of François Rabbath at the bass. It is about a father writing a letter of advice to his young daughter. I always sing along with this passage:

> *Nunca te entregues ni te apartes*
> *junto al camino nunca digas*
> *no puedo más y aquí me quedo*
> *y aquí me quedo.*
>
> *Never give up, never fall apart,*
> *in the middle of the road never say*
> *I can't go on and I'm staying here*
> *I'm staying here.*

Funny, it's when I *stop* running that I suddenly feel like an outlaw "on the run."

My edict is *"Keep going!"*

But if I lose hope—if you lose hope—we can no longer journey. That is because passion—that elusive blend of joie de vivre and desire for exploration and conquest that was pushing us—is gone. With our motor taken away, our heart quits. We are lost; we give up.

I have read—is it true?—that sometimes humans die if they give up their will to live.

Some animals in captivity do as well.

The image implied by the expression *to give up* is wrong. You are not putting anything up. You are not presenting the gods with a sacrificial offering that you're holding high above your head for all to see, for some sacred giant multicolored bird to swoop down and carry away into golden clouds, grazing your head in the process.

By giving up, you're actually *putting down* what you were carrying—a project, a quest, a dream. You're not only dropping it on the ground but burying it deep, then throwing earth on top and smoothing the surface with your foot, attempting to erase any trace of what lies below. You're *giving down*.

But.

It is not over.

At the end of the tunnel

Forget the dream?

I've tried that.

I told you how, right after my arrest at the top of WTC, utterly destroyed, I moved on to other goals for a short while. But WTC refused to disappear from my horizon. So I gave up giving up.

Let's eviscerate the multiheaded creatures that attack our dream the second we're convinced they're real. Rebel against doom by refusing to accept reality! **Surprise yourself!**

Come to the edge.
We might fall.
Come to the edge.
It's too high!
COME TO THE EDGE!
And they came,
And he pushed,
*And they flew.**

Besides reminding me of a baby bird's first flying lesson—pushed out of the nest by its parents—this poem promises that an imaginary "fear-to-dream" line of thought exists. The fear of what's on the other side should not prevent you from trespassing over the line. Or walking the line, if you're able.

The courage to keep going

My inclination is rarely to switch forcefully from fear to its opposite, *courage*, even though to me they seem cast from the same mold. Instead, armed with poetry and cunning, I launch myself into a kind of "soft hunting" for courage, more of an investigation actually.

Courage—for me, another human distortion!

I have little use for something I do not comprehend; I find the common definition of courage too simplistic, so I layer it with provocation, determination and tenacity.

*Christopher Logue, "Come to the Edge," from *New Numbers* (London: Jonathan Cape, 1969), pp. 65–66.

If courage is colored by tenacity, as I believe, then let's reinvent the notion of courage.

A courageous attitude would be not to condemn yourself for failure, but to respond to its duress. Gather what can be used to bring salvation. Orchestrate a reversal of fortune.

The lion tamer at the circus does not discuss the risks of his profession. But the audience does. It promulgates the cliché that fear is healthy. "If you're not scared, you're in mortal danger!" The lesson that popular un-wisdom espouses is "Be afraid; it will help you."

Nonsense!

But if you focus on your own imperfections, gather what prevents you from progressing and can convert misfortune into its opposite, then, yes, you are saving yourself from being eaten alive by lions.

"I have not failed. I've just found ten thousand ways that won't work," as Thomas Edison was wont to say.

Here is a tale of redemption I picked up when watching the thrilling movie *Apollo 13*.

Captain James Lovell recalls a time when he was piloting a Banshee airplane over the Sea of Japan. Because it was in combat conditions, his aircraft carrier had no running lights. But his radar had jammed and his homing signal did not work, so his plane was drifting away from the invisible carrier somewhere on the big dark ocean.

He switched on his map light, but that created a short that caused the entire instrument panel to disappear and plunged the cockpit into darkness; he could not even read his altitude.

And he knew he was running out of fuel.

Thinking about ditching, he looked down at the darkness and noticed a green trail that looked like "a long carpet." It was the phosphorescent substance produced by algae that powerful ships churn in their wake, and it lighted the way straight to the carrier. "If my cockpit lights hadn't shorted out, I never would have seen it!" the captain said.

Seeking other points of view on courage, I found:

Courage is almost a contradiction in terms. It means a strong desire to live taking the form of readiness to die.
• G. K. CHESTERTON

Creativity requires the courage to let go of certainties.
• ERICH FROMM

Keep your fears to yourself; share your courage with others.
• ROBERT LOUIS STEVENSON

I take my hat down—no, my friends always correct me: "In America you say: *I take my hat off*"—and I take my hat off as well (I have many hats)—for one artist in particular: the talented young juggler known as Basile Dragon (Cyril Rabbath, son of the genius double-bass interpreter, composer and teacher François Rabbath).

When I met Cyril at Rue Laplace two years ago, he joyfully confided a courageous and creative decision he had just acted upon.

He felt he had come to a point in his professional life where drastic changes were going to be spectacularly beneficial to his art. He had finished burning his collection of practice-diaries (as I watched him calmly juggle eight balls at once, I could only imagine how many precious thoughts he had jotted down on the way to such achievements). He abandoned the style he had worked so hard to master. *And* he changed his stage name.

My friend told me all that with pride and a grand smile of humbleness.

It was with the same pride and elation that I wrote *WTC "New Organisation"* (with the French *s*, not the American *z*) on the cover of a freshly acquired blank book, to resume the gathering of data, interrupted by my arrest. That simple act of calligraphy was to lead to the walk. I literally danced around, telling everyone (including myself) that I was back on the insane project and that "this time it's going to happen!"

I suddenly felt that it was my words Churchill had stolen.

"Success is not final, failure is not fatal: it is the courage to continue that counts." And, "If you're going through hell, keep going."

I had been slogging deep in muddy ruts, but now I sensed they were turning dry, then rising off the ground into steel tracks. I followed their shiny parallelism (akin to twin towers) and knew that the end of the tunnel was near. Its cold walls were growing warm: I saw the sun rising. I heard birds. I smelled a fresh breeze rekindling the embers of my dream.

One more note: in times of distress, or on the recovery road from failure and despair, it helps to seek support from other artists by reviewing the achievements that have resulted from their own hundred-year wars.

When I need such a boost, I invariably read Christo's accounts of how most of his projects became reality only after dozens of years of red tape and bureaucracy. As I read, I hear a faint voice deep inside me singing joyfully: "See. It can be done!"

Quick! Join me in recomposing the balance lost. Let's move on. Or as the head of the SWAT team shouts: *"Go, go, go, go, go, go!"*

Celebration is in order, but instead of opening a bottle of Champagne on a rooftop, I place myself imaginatively at the bottom of one of my three favorite staircases in the world: the unimaginable Chand Baori stepwell in India, built in the tenth century to store water.

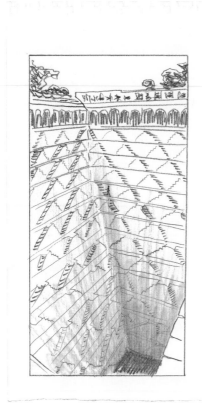

(The other two are the 487 steps carved into a rock cliff in the Elbsandsteingebirge near Dresden, Germany, in the thirteenth century, and a series of flat stones sticking out of an indestructible wall overhanging an abyss on the Inca Trail somewhere between Cuzco and Machu Picchu.)

Standing at the well's bottom, thirty meters deep, I look at the 3,500 steps geometrically surrounding me, I choose one of the multiple ascent routes and I start climbing.

If you are down, I invite you to explore the website Taringa!, which lists the fifteen most famous staircases in the world,* and choose the stairs you'd like to climb back to the surface.

*http://www.taringa.net/posts/imagenes/16294559/Escaleras-del-mundo-JD.html.

Climbing up is a sure way to experience in body language the resurgence from doom. Because climbing is deeply rooted in all of us by nature, it could mean—for me, it does mean—that we are all inextinguishable optimists. Even though we tend to forget it.

I never go too long without visiting some skyscraper's rooftop. My blood needs to breathe the clouds.

Son of an aviator,* I always keep in mind my father's comment that preceded my *baptême de l'air* (maiden airplane trip) on a double-decker Bréguet, when I was twelve: "To take off you must place yourself against the wind."

Which means there are times when you need to ask a potentially devastating force to befriend you for a moment—a very decisive moment.

*Colonel Edmond Petit (1914–2000) was a pilot-observer during World War II, a writer, a historian, a poet, a sportsman, a linguist, a translator, a theatrical director, a digger of escape tunnels, an art critic, a book reviewer, a lecturer and by his own admission . . . a purist.

(((((((((Surprise yourself!   )))))))))

When I *feel* the situation is hopeless, when I *believe* I cannot over-come, I surprise myself by challenging what I am feeling and believing.

Feel? Believe?

What if these impressions do not reflect reality? I could be mistaking the situation; I could be misjudging my capacities.

Just in case, my swift response is invariably to embrace the opposite of my former feelings and beliefs: "There *are* solutions; I *have* the force to fight."

Then I go on, decidedly, and mold a different reality!

Although I keep a large dose of "surprise yourself" on hand to counter adversity (my self-defense type of creativity), I reserve another large amount to joyfully surprise myself at all times. When you surprise yourself, you surprise others—a ripple effect of creativity.

Take laughter, for instance. I admire its contagiousness. A man starts laughing at a crowded tramway stop and soon even the most serious of commuters is catching the virus: half smiles develop inexorably into the entire group bursting with uncontrollable joy!*

When I entertain myself by looking at the world in surprising ways—which comes naturally—it never fails to enrich me! Often on a whim, I'll enter the kind of store that holds absolutely no appeal to me: an

---

*http://www.upworthy.com/watch-this-dude-infect-people-at-a-bus-stop-and-see-if-youre-susceptible?c=ufb1.

auto-body shop, a jewelry outlet, a fishing store . . . and I'll come out with a new idea concerning a magic trick or a lock-picking tool!

I'm also in the habit of paging through a magazine backward, to keep the element of surprise alive. Or in a waiting room, I'll stare at the ceiling (that too proves to be highly contagious) and imagine the ceiling as the floor of a new apartment! I picture myself entering the room, careful not to trip on the foot-high threshold and stepping over the white beams that here and there cross my path.

(My predilection for ceilings collects amused frowns from visitors: in my house there are objects glued to the ceilings and framed photographs held flat against them.)

My overall inclination to surprise myself has translated into daily unconscious creative exercises: I can't resist experimenting, even briefly, with the opposite or the mirror image of a concept.

Imagine my satisfaction in stumbling upon this new take on "The Princess and the Pea" (by Lola Gruber, in a Hermès publicity brochure): *"There once was a garden pea that was hypersensitive to noise. Every night it piled ten mattresses and a princess on its head, but still it couldn't sleep."*

I find that surprising myself is a powerful creative motor.

Try it.

If you work in an office, take off your shoes and socks, and walk around barefoot! I know it's silly, but you know what? Two things will happen.

First, you'll have a whole new set of sensations. For the first time you'll appreciate how soft the hall carpet is, how warm the wooden floor is in the reception area; you'll be tickled by the granulated freshness of the rough concrete in the kitchenette.

Second, you will be amazed at how unobservant your fellow employees are: most of them will keep at their daily tasks and—I assure you—entirely miss the fact that you are . . . "on your skin" (as a wire-walker I prefer that expression to "barefoot").

When you go back home, try this: from the moment you arrive at your door, deprive yourself of one sense. Say, your sense of sight. Close your eyes.

You may fumble with your keys for a moment, but you will find the right one by its familiar shape and weight. You also know the number of steps to your apartment door—and if you don't know the exact number, it doesn't matter, because your legs will remember. Once inside, the many other little tasks you have to go through—blind—will provide more minute challenges that can be overcome easily by leaning on your other senses.

Surprised, that you managed to accomplish everything?

From time to time, throw in the little intermission of surprising yourself in the course of your week!

For example, eat your soup and brush your teeth with "the other hand."

And now let's make a fool of ourselves together.

On the count of three, let's burst out laughing! Ready?

One . . .

Two . . .

Three!

Ha-ha-ha-ha-ha-ha-ha-ha-ha, ho, ho, ho! Hi! Hi-hi-hi-ho, ha-ha!

Good . . .

Don't you feel better?

(((((((((((((((((•)))))))))))))))))

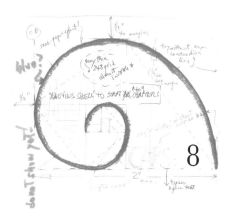

8   THE COUP

Plans and solutions are far behind.

Failure, forgotten.

Danger is real, fear a choice. I face into the wind and boost my reactors. Take-off is imminent.

There is no return

Imagine, at dawn, atop the South Tower: I place my left foot on the cable; I'm about to step onto the high wire.

I have penetrated the lion's den.

I have reached a point of no return. There will be more!

My points of no return are just that: points. As tiny as a pin's head, with no room for reason to stand on top! These points are where intuition takes over.

My intuition does not need standing room; it hovers lightly and twirls like a breeze at the edge of a precipice.

Decisively I will place my other foot on the wire.

Just as decisively, when I start writing, I commit myself to an opening sentence, then I add another, and another, until I have an opening paragraph.

I walk. I write. Whatever the scene of creative struggle may be, I execute the creative crime.

As far as I'm concerned, the artistic crime I committed at WTC, which I call the Coup, reached its initial point of no return when the delivery van in which I was hiding with one ton of equipment left the horizontality of Lower Manhattan traffic to descend the ramp that led to the underground entrances of the South Tower freight elevators.

My frame of mind?

Today I'm going to break laws!

As if it were not enough to act upon a spectacular disrespect for *gravity*— a law of nature—I was carrying my tradition of disregard for the laws of humans to new heights, in this instance by having naively forgotten all along to ask for a permit to set a wire between the highest towers in the world!

This is what happened.

After hours of uncertainty, my equipment, my crew and I are finally allowed to step inside a cavernous plywood box that hangs on cables. We are lucky: it is the last freight elevator ride of the day!

An impatient foreman shouts: "Which floor?"

"104!" I reply.

In a flash, the secret plan I have worked on for so long no longer stands! Instead of ascending to the eighty-second floor, where an accomplice and a hiding place await us, I am now going for the highest level this elevator can reach—only because I have just noticed a little pencil scribbling on the plywood above my head: "0-104."

As always, there is a thin line between intuition and improvisation. And as a wire-walker, I see them both balancing on that same thin line!

Survival mode

Inside the freight elevator, which shoots upward at tremendous speed, I spend one second questioning my sanity. "What now? There is no Plan B!" The air around me compresses, as does time—maybe the effect of acceleration? It triggers an alarming mutation: I transform into a wild animal fixated on survival . . . of the project.

When I am that wild animal, with the life of my dream at stake, I am able to anticipate intuition!

The following did not happen. I dreamed it.

Someone is coming at me with a gun in a dark alley. He orders me to surrender my wallet—or better, something priceless to me: an attaché case containing the files of a new project.

I have an advantage. My assailant does not know I'm ready to die for my possession. "No! You won't get anything from me!" I say calmly.

Second advantage: I'm not afraid of death. "Shoot me if you must!" I add.

And lastly (enormous advantage): I am curious. What leads a person to the brink of taking another's life?

Survival prompts an improvised lie as misdirection: "Hey, this is a great gun, I have the same model! But you know, I have a problem with the safety; it is not well designed, because when you . . ."

I end up inviting the "bad guy" to dinner and get more of my questions answered . . . that's my daydream!

At the boundary of life and death, at the moment of truth, creativity becomes life. What I do then is simple: I reach the essence of my effort and constantly reaffirm its validity. To go through a task of immense proportion, I follow its complexity, embrace its tension, and invent new possibilities every second. The resulting blend becomes the lung of the operation—I breathe through it.

Maybe what I just described is the opposite of panic.

I'm quick to use the word *survival* whenever embellishments and details are set aside to get directly to the core.

In survival mode, I zero in on what is essential: my idea, my action, my project. And I do not let it go. From that point on, my focus, my energy, my creative mechanisms are guided by what is paramount: the urge to keep going, to survive, to succeed. At that moment I cannot fail—and the absolute commitment *not* to fail transforms me into a predator, hunting, scanning left and right for anything that can delay—or impede—my relentless stalking of my target.

. . . We land on the 104th floor (a deserted slab still under construction). We hide, we wait for darkness. Only then can we bring the equipment to the roof.

The instant I pass my head through the concrete opening, fresh, crisp air slaps me brutally in the face. But what assails me has nothing to do with a burst of breeze from high altitude. A split-second look at the roof across the void reveals another of Murphy's poisoned gifts.

In the weeks since I last visited, the aluminum panels that will ultimately adorn the entire perimeter of the building's crown and permanently cover its steel skeleton have been installed, faster than I anticipated. Several steel beams that I had planned to use to anchor my cavalettis are no longer visible!

I have no choice now but to spend a significant part of the allotted rigging time to improvise a technical solution; equipment will have to be remeasured and rearranged. The coup might fail.

Hours later, I notice the elevator that brings construction workers to the roof has been put in motion. I instantly cut short the finishing touches of the rigging.

No time to think.

Too late for questions.

Mental and physical exhaustion from the last twenty hours of my adventure assails me, a paralyzing lethargy creeps over me. I shake it off like wet dogs do.

Frantic, I change into my costume as fast as I can.

Instead of drinking my little remaining water, I use it to clean my hands and face.

I wobble to the corner where the cable impatiently awaits.

The cable is definitely not well installed.

Fighting the impossible

. . . 1,350 feet high, on my windy roof corner, bereft of energy, betrayed by time, doubting for a second any balance left in me, I remain indecisive, maybe on the verge of panic, a thick morsel of bitterness in my mouth.

Yet I grab the balancing-pole.

Yet I place one foot on the thin steel cable, the other on the giant steel tower.

In that compromising position, I suddenly understand why I can't place my other foot on the cable: the Impossible has grabbed the pole as well! But I violently reject its claim.

If there had been a movie camera shooting the scene (I had rented one, but it was not used), you would see clearly that I shook the pole with some sort of fury.

In my book *To Reach the Clouds* and in interviews, I explain that gesture as a habitual one. When I lift the pole before each of my crossings, I claim, "I always jounce it, maneuver it between my fingers to find its center, to accustom my arms to its weight."

No one ever doubted me, but what I said was a lie.

What I was doing—what I do before each of my crossings, but have never told a soul until now—is fight the Impossible.

I fight the Impossible until it releases its grip and flies away.

IMPOSSIBLE: not a master word, just a master.

From when I was young, the building of the great pyramids of Egypt fascinated me. I knew they were made of huge blocks of stone too heavy for me to move. But part of a block, a small rock, I could hold in my cupped hands. And I could see how that rock is composed of grains of sand, is it not? And a pinch of sand I can impose my will upon—can I not? That morsel I can displace and dispose of as I wish. I can even blow it away and force it to fly!

From then on, whenever a task of gargantuan proportions rises in front of me, I do not dwell upon its magnitude. I immediately break it into tiny parts that make my goal manageable. (On the high wire, this process is inescapable because one step at a time is a must!) In this way, the impossible becomes nothing more than a prodigious collection of minute fistfuls of possibilities, a series of steps, pieces of a puzzle awaiting assembly.

Not overwhelming in the least—in fact, promising playfulness!

But the master has another face. That of a cruel and vicious dictator who acts with no holds barred.

This face shows itself during any coup when, for example, I must carry out an action that I no longer have time to perform.

This type of incapacity triggers an instant loss of hope; yet, surprisingly, it is the very force of my despair—a raging rebellion—that prevents me from giving up.

. . . Fortunately I'm not the only one struggling. The pole is on my side and resists being taken away as well.

Ultimately, we win the fight—we always do—and as the long bar returns to my sole grip, it gives me some of the faith it has stored up prior to our crossings and lends me, discreetly, some of the balance of which it is made.

I grab that faith, I take in that balance. Just as I now grab the pole, with new-found strength. Doubts evaporate. The pole and I are about to perform a successful and magnificent first crossing. I turn that belief into absolute certainty as I set my other foot onto the cable.

(I open parentheses here to let you know that this complicity happens with any of my props before a performance, especially if adversity has settled in. May you profit from such partnership in crime as well!)

Inside the first step

When I take that first step on the wire, I feel like the writer who, after much work and countless attempts, finally embraces with joyful confidence the opening to his novel and abandons it to the page.

In fact, I collect book openings I find delightfully intriguing! Here, for you, are some of my favorites:

> *In eighteenth-century France there lived a man who was one of the most gifted and abominable personages in an era that knew no lack of gifted and abominable personages.*
>
> • PATRICK SÜSKIND, *PERFUME*

> *Lolita, light of my life, fire of my loins. My sin, my soul. Lo-lee-ta: the tip of the tongue taking a trip of three steps down the palate to tap, at three, on the teeth. Lo. Lee. Ta.*
>
> • VLADIMIR NABOKOV, *LOLITA*

> *In the* Abalone *(Arizona)* Morning Tribune *for August third there appeared on page five an advertisement eight columns wide and twenty-one inches long. In type faces grading from small pica to ninety-six point the advertisement told of a circus to be held in Abalone that day, the tents to be spread upon a vacant field on the banks of the Santa Ana River, a bald spot in the city's growth surrounded by all manner of houses and habitations.*
>
> • CHARLES G. FINNEY, *THE CIRCUS OF DR. LAO*

The sky was a donkey's swollen paunch hanging threateningly low overhead. The warm, sticky wind swept up the scattered leaves and violently shook the stunted banana trees that graced the front of the town hall.

> • LUIS SEPÚLVEDA, *THE OLD MAN WHO READ LOVE STORIES*

"Three examples are enough!" Kurt Wüermli, my personal assistant of yester-year, used to remind me. And when I'd answer, "*No, no, no, no, no!*" he'd remonstrate: "One *no*—even without an exclamation point—does the job."

I also take delight in gathering great musical openings—the kind of bold and thrilling first notes, first steps, that make it impossible to leave the concert hall. Here—for Kurt—three examples only:

- "The Man with the Harmonica," by Ennio Morricone (from the film *Once Upon a Time in the West* by Sergio Leone)—*a sustained line of coarse, high-pitched plaint.*

- "Balada Conducatorolui," by Sapo Perapaskero with the Taraf de Haïdouks (from the film *Latcho Drom* by Tony Gatlif)—*an opening phrase that introduces screeching sounds from a broken one-string violin.*

- And the outrageous cadenza of clarinet that sounds to me like a shrieking New York siren metamorphoses into the rich opening of George Gershwin's "Rhapsody in Blue."

The question of how to begin an action, how to start a performance, captivates me, for it triggers rich lessons in creativity.

That first step, an essential moment, a point of no return I call *attack*, was the theme of a weeklong seminar I gave at Oberlin College.

I made a point of delivering my welcome speech—the seminar's attack—while walking around nonstop with my students inside an assembly hall! The walking was an improvised exercise, which I thought would surprise the students and wake them up—and after all, what better way to start a First Step seminar than by walking?

Then I challenged each of them to improvise a two-minute presentation featuring a memorable and inspiring "first time"—pleasant or not. (One young man shed all his clothes in front of us, proudly sharing how great he felt to have finally accepted to pose naked for an art class.)

Next I asked them to come up with an ideal "first step way" to introduce someone to becoming a blacksmith, a mortician, or a tango dancer! I made them explain their choices.

They discovered the convincing power focused improvisation can have on people. (Perhaps inspired by the walking speech, one young woman took my hand and pulled me into a little potpourri dance while explaining why the tango is the best dance!)

In further sessions, we investigated dramatically different styles of diving into a situation.

We impersonated a maestro crossing the stage of a concert hall and sitting down at the piano, and a parent delivering ransom to a kidnapper. We studied the pratfall with which Buster Keaton often entered a room, and then we practiced it, complete with its immediate follow-up—looking back at the floor to see what had caused the tripping (an essential detail that lends veracity to the attacking move).

From making the first step to crossing an abyss, for me, professionally, there is usually not much transition! Nonetheless, by the end of the week I had managed to bring my students near the brink, to have them consider what the hardest project in the world could entail.

Facing the impossible

. . . After losing its grip on my balancing-pole, the Impossible flew across to the North Tower, where it now sits, tauntingly waiting for me.

I begin my crossing looking the Impossible in the eyes.

The bullfighter enters the arena, his eyes riveted on the bull's eyes.

That's how I negotiate any struggle against all odds.

I keep eye contact and I inch my way one step at a time.

I exercise caution with extreme certainty.

I produce solidity.

That's how I begin writing a book, too, and that's how I keep going. I live through any art as if it were a wire-walk, as if my life depended on it.

I create in survival mode!

Cheating the impossible

. . . Oh . . . no . . . this is the worst rigged wire I've ever set foot on!

The Impossible spreads its presence!

It has advanced from the arrival point to the halfway point of the crossing; it has invaded the middle of the void, where my wire is at its most sensitive, where wind and vibrations plot to be deadly.

I know very well what to do.

If taking the first step is facing the impossible, taking the second step is cheating the impossible.

In anything I do, the only way for me to succeed is to keep going, as if the Impossible is not watching! I ignore its presence and busy myself in gaining cable, gaining pages, gaining progress.

. . . Step by step—but with steps now grown fluid and expansive—I cut through the morning breeze.

I pass the middle. I have pierced the armor of the Impossible.

I smile: I know I will get to the other side. Caution gives way to elation.

An elation into which I sense it is deadly to surrender. Thus I collect all the calm I can find from the sky, from the void, from my wire, from my balancing-pole . . . and I keep walking, adding elegance to this first crossing.

And then, with the smile of one elongated last step, I accost the North Tower that has allowed itself to be conquered.

Ultimately, I'll promenade (or dance, as some witnesses remember it) from one end of the cable to the other, back and forth for a long time—for an infinity of joy—and together all of those walks will be remembered as The Walk.

Now what should I tell you?

That you should attempt one day to fight, face and cheat the impossible; and that you might discover it's not impossible!

Attempt? Actually, no. The artist's efforts should never have the color of an attempt. I don't try; I succeed.

And yet, joining in the mad, unwavering fury to win is one essential quality I have not yet mentioned.

Humility

Even when I have triumphed against formidable forces—even when I have dismissed warnings of "It cannot be done, don't even try!"—I know I am not invincible.

I learned from Papa Rudy how several wire-walkers lost their lives: toward the end of a crossing, as they saw the arrival platform draw near, their faith in their success extended to the deadly point when, still on the wire, three feet from landing, they believed they had successfully walked across! In that vision of *the last step*, they grew overconfident, lacked attention . . . and missed the wire just before they would have landed!

This is why humility—a virtue that is so hard for me to maintain—must be cultivated by the imaginative artist. Humility will keep you alive, not just physically but creatively alive. It will bring you back to the purity (again, to the core) of what you are constructing. It will keep you in joy and richness while stripping you of unnecessary subterfuges and adornments.

But once you have achieved the unachievable, should you fear retaliation or punishment for your dare?

Fear not!

The Impossible can't retaliate—you just proved it does not exist. That you had better believe!

Faith

Faith: what replaces doubt in *my* dictionary. Indeed, I have crossed out certain words in the thick printed volume of my existence—and with the same fat red pen, I have circled others with an aureole. (I make saints out of some of my words.)

The faith I draw upon to carry my life in my hands across the abyss is akin to religious faith.

My religion has a three-part creed.

First.

I believe in myself—which, by the way, is a sign of strength, not ego.

I would not perform the first step of a crossing if I didn't carry beforehand (beforefoot) the certainty of the arrival step. Otherwise, I would run away in cowardice.

Each time I aim too high, I have the stubbornness to believe that I possess the strength that allows me to overcome extreme difficulty. Each time, though I have no experience or proof of its existence, I find myself trusting—as a matter of faith—that the force is dormant inside me. All I need do is wake it up!

Once, a long time ago, I visited the French province of Brittany with my daughter, Cordia-Gypsy, and her mother, Elaine. Gypsy, carried around in a wicker basket, was then a six-month-old being devouring the countryside with wide, hungry eyes.

My photographer friend Thierry Orbach offers us a taste of the sea in his little sailboat. The ocean seems unwilling; it grunts and growls and groans and gurgles. And nearby, a lurking storm shows its teeth. I'm terrified (my excuses are that I don't know anything about sailing other than a few hundred knots, I don't like endless deep water, and I can barely swim). But with adventurous Thierry all smiles, Elaine and I muster an enthusiastic "Yes!"

Quickly the coastline disappears, and we find ourselves storm-tossed in every direction. I know that Thierry, a master sailor, knows perfectly well what he is doing; nevertheless, I'm convinced we are on our way to the bottom of the sea. Elaine kneels on the deck to keep her balance while clinging to "Gypoo" for dear life.

Thierry skillfully guides the boat through a razor comb of sharp rocks mere feet under the surface, but the storm drowns out his words: "Coming about—watch the boom!" so when the horizontal spar swings around, it barely misses Gypsy. That's when I declare in no uncertain terms that I have had enough of this hell ride and ask Thierry to get us to the nearest landing.

Twenty seasick minutes later, parents and child are two feet away from the foot of a giant ladder anchored in a twenty-foot-high stone wall washed by the waves. Between the rocking of the boat, the growing rain, and the crudeness of the ladder—the rungs are unusually far apart—we are facing a slippery obstacle on a survival parkour.

Flashes of lightning slash the growing darkness—there's no time for me to rig a lifesaving system.

I wrap Gypsy in a swath of blanket and cuddle her snuggly in the basket of my left arm and start to ascend the ladder.

But you need two arms to climb a ladder!

To protect the life of my child, I must do what can't be done.

I grab one rung with my right hand and then let go of my grip for the split second it takes to launch myself upward in midair before I close my fingers on the next wet rung too far away! I pause to adjust my delicate balance, to reaffirm the hold on my precious human cargo. Then I lunge again for the next rung, which I grip with fingers of steel.

As the waves underneath us foam and welter, I repeat this extremely chancy acrobatic move ten times in a row. Each time with success because of the focus, strength and determination leading my effort. And because, to save Gypsy, I have no choice but to succeed.

Ten minutes later, parents and child celebrate being alive in a nearby *crêperie bretonne*, with a delightful *cidre brut*.

But all these years later, that short climb remains the most demanding, frightening and daring physical action of my entire life; and I am reminded of what Robert Bresson wrote in his shooting journal: "The greater the success, the closer it verges upon failure."*

Second.

I believe in outside forces and influences, I believe in the personality of the elements, I believe in the aliveness of things seemingly inanimate.

You already know of my belief that certain objects have a soul: my top hat, my three juggling balls and my steel wire-rope. I also recognize the aliveness of certain other man-made structures (a cathedral, a skyscraper) as well as nature's creations (trees, mountains, waterfalls).

I am convinced that what surrounds us sometimes emits secret messages that beg to be deciphered, for our own good—to guide us, to help us, to protect us.

This is why I wrote a chapter titled "Meeting the Gods" in the book on my WTC walk. In it, I recall how I summoned the air, the void, the towers, the wire, the balancing-pole, even my slippers, to lend their assertive presence to my journey. To add their godlike powers to the walk.

In my opinion, not all objects have life. But I am convinced that the ones that do, receive that life from us. The baton of a (possessed) orchestra conductor, the chisel of a (transcendental) sculptor, the balancing-pole of an (illuminated) wire-walker . . .

*Bresson, *Notes on the Cinematographer*.

Part of my faith is to acknowledge that the faith lent to me by these elements or objects is going to serve my pursuit rather than turn against it!

To protect that faith, I never insult these "sacred beings" by openly denying their aliveness. When a moment of doubt concerning their existence arises, I keep it secret.

(By the way, one of my embarrassing weaknesses is to believe that a shadow carries a fraction of the life of the person or object to which it is shackled. Therefore, as a matter of poetic, surreal courtesy, I avoid gratuitously stepping on a shadow! If you see me tiptoeing and playing leapfrog in a tree-lined alley of a park, it is probably because the ground is carpeted by dozens of dancing shadows from the branches above!)

Third.

I believe in the unbelievable.

The natural flow of this discourse leads to this not-so-distant belief.

Consider (even if only for an instant) believing in myths, miracles and magic.

I have praised the virtues of simplicity, of elegance. I should add that I find a certain intellectual elegance in simply believing. In believing in simple things, and believing in them with simplicity, with purity.

One of the creative forces that never fails to empower my endeavors is to allow myths, fairy tales, miracles, mythology, magic, mysteries, the wonders of legends, even old traditions or proverbs to enter my life and feed my creativity.

(Parentheses here to salute "impossible things": things, objects—and, why not, animals or people—that carry within them a mystery that seems impossible to decode. I make sure my life is kept on a razor's edge of excitement and intrigue by surrounding myself with such **mysterious objects**.)

It may amuse you that I believe that long, long ago, we were given the ability to dive into the deepest seas, to fly, to penetrate fire, to possess ten senses, to impose upon the elements. But over time, because we started using less of these gifts, and less frequently (or misusing them), they dulled out and vanished (or were taken from us).

Proof?

From time to time an earthling is able to visit another planet, to dive without equipment deep into the sea, to enter a volcano's fire-spitting mouth, to crawl inside the deepest cave, to fly wingless, to walk between mountains on a line barely existing.

At times, place your faith in the improbable, in the not yet proven, in what legends are made of.

My intimate encounters with this far-fetched side of creativity suggest that it can help you to push beyond the limits of our human condition to discover that sometimes what is unauthenticated is, in fact . . . true!

Believe . . . Believe . . . in the long-forgotten fact that we humans can perform what is deemed unachievable.

((((((((mysterious objects   ))))))))

Allow me to transport you to one of the world's most isolated inhabited islands: Easter Island, famous for its mysterious and stunning sacred stone monoliths called *moai*, which were made between AD 1250 and 1500.

Mysterious mostly because unanswered questions abound about the statues, many of which are more than fifteen feet tall and weigh more than fifteen tons.

How were they carved? The inhabitants of the island—the Rapa Nui—did not have metal chisels at the time.

How were they transported from the quarry—sometimes a distance of five kilometers—to the ceremonial sites where they were left standing, facing inland? The wheel was unknown to the Rapa Nui—and if the *moai* had been pulled over rolling logs—as some say—why is there no trace of a forest?

How were they erected in place without a block and tackle to pull the ropes? The pulley had not yet appeared on the island and there was no mechanical equipment . . .

I lost myself in fascination reading accounts of explorations and studies concerning the *moai*. Eventually, I became familiar with the work of Thor Heyerdahl, the explorer of *Kon-Tiki* fame.

When he visited the island, having no written history to lean on, he kept asking the people he met: "How did your ancestors move the *moai*?" Toward the end of his research, an illustrious elder provided the answer with a smile: "They walked!"

Soon thereafter, the theory was tested. A mock-up of a statue was made and set standing. With the help of a rather small group of volunteers, some strong ropes, and trial and error, the top of the heavy statue was tilted first to the left, then to the right, in such a way that its base, pivoting slightly with each move, managed to creep forward. Soon, as the maneuver became more efficient, the monolith was taking regular "steps" forward and had advanced a good number of yards.

The Rapa Nui elder was right: they walked!

I try not to surround myself with only answers and certitudes. I invite mysteries to live with me—sometimes tangibly!

Behind the chessboard in my living room stands a strange-looking contraption, which I call the Mysterious Object.

It is a pointed wooden cylinder, four inches in diameter and seven inches tall, that houses inside each of two opposite grooves a curved

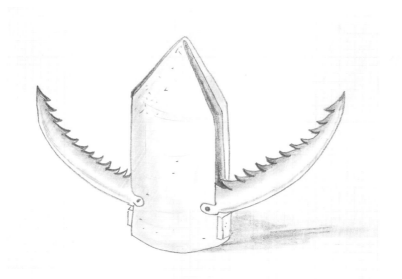

arm of metal with sharp teeth. The two arms remain in a spread-out position, but you can also push them back into their respective grooves, and hold them flush with the body of the cylinder with one hand. If you let go, a strong spring throws them back instantly and aggressively into the spread-out position.

My father found the object in the attic of an old family-château in the center of France and had it dated to before the 1789 Revolution. But despite years of research and endless inquiries in multiple fields, he could not get a satisfying explanation for the precise use of the object, which looks and acts like a weapon or a trap. I took over my father's quest and keep asking for an answer. Can you give it to me?

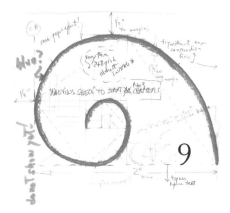

9 | AFTERMATH

What happens after you achieve the unachievable?

Your friends, along with the rest of the world, congratulate you. You are given novel opportunities, you receive numerous propositions, a sense of urgency imposes itself on you.

Everyone asks, "What's next?" Or worse, urges you to surpass yourself on the spot: "How are you going to top that?"

Hold it right there!

First, first.

Rest and celebrate! (I'm known to do both at the same time.)

Enjoy your joy, be proud of your pride.

Without any false modesty, toreros use the word *triumph* to describe a successful bullfight: *"Ayer he triunfado en Barcelona!"* (Yesterday I had a triumph in Barcelona!) Why should a lesser term be used to refer to forty thousand people rising to their feet and screaming their admiration?

For the felicity of storytelling, relive the event and pass around the details. For the solidity of documenting, ask witnesses for testimonies and collect their memories. Who knows, you might want to write a book about it someday!

Yes, look back and be amazed at what you did. And . . . don't forget to be a bit terrified as well.

Rest and celebrate, we agree; but keep both short-lived.

How to pick up the roses

Let's back up a second.

Is there a *right way* to face the bravos? I believe so.

I face the bravos with the same daring spirit that earlier made me face the impossible, because congratulations are dangerous.

They always agree.

They do not deliver the annoyances critics do.

In a sense, they're useless.

Don't be automatically, immediately satisfied.

Collect kudos with your heart, not with avid open hands. The heart has a more subtle and selective way of receiving and storing such delicate and ultimately treacherous goods.

Let's return to our seats on the perimeter of the bullfighting ring for a moment to watch the *maestro* begin his *vuelta* (the circular tour of triumph that ends a *corrida de toros*). He parades, smiling, along the wooden *barreras*, presenting to the crowd a frozen hand salute, while gifts are thrown into the arena in homage to his talent and courage: silk scarves, men's hats, cigars and a shower of red roses!

What a lesson in theatrical presence, when the torero suspends his walk for a second, without breaking the fluidity of his victory stride, in order to pick up a single flower amid the dozens lying there.

Actually, Rudolf Nureyev remains for me the ultimate Maestro of picking up roses from the stage: during his encores, the dancer continued to keep his eyes glued to his adoring, entranced audience, yet he must have snapped a mental photograph of the floor from the corner of one eye, because out of the multitude of flowers carpeting the stage he was always able to pick up one without looking—the most beautiful one—and present it to the audience as a reciprocal homage.

Accept the awards presented to you but do not ask for them. Add them to your collection if you wish, frame them if you must, but do not contemplate your reflection in the glass pane and do not hang them in the Hall of Fame of your memory.

Pinned to my bathroom wall is the *arrêté* (fancy French word for "decision") proclaiming my being made a Chevalier de l'Ordre des Arts et des Lettres by France's Minister of Culture. It reminds me daily of the false promises made by power-thirsty civil servants the world over . . . *Pfft!*

(Here's a digression I can't help offering.

"Pfft!" is one of the correct ways of describing the sound a French magician makes when vanishing a card.

The American equivalent would be *"Zap!"* or *"Presto!"* What about in Thai? Well, writers of action scenes, magical and otherwise, wait no longer. There

exists a dictionary of onomatopoeia.* Go find it,
then—*takoom!*—buy it.
And—*ba-da-bing!*—you'll
swear by it whenever you're
in search of the best noise
for your helicopter hit by
lightning, your gun accidentally firing, your parrot
yawning out of lack of conversation, or your . . . No!
Three examples are enough!)

Mute triumph

Kudos and awards . . . or
else: the absence thereof.

Nothing.

Silence!

Your achievement went unnoticed. Your expectations were not fulfilled. The
effect of receiving the opposite of accolades will be negligible (and bearable)
if you instantly remind yourself of the truth you carry in your heart: you did
what you did.

You swam the Channel, but no one witnessed your arrival? So be it. Send
kudos to yourself. Calligraph a certificate and frame it.

In a sense you have been lucky: you won't be tempted by foolish invitations
to sell your soul!

KA-BOOM! A Dictionary of Comic Book Words, Symbols and Onomatopoeia by Kevin Taylor
(lulu.com, 2007).

The perils of success

You disagree with the incoming opportunities? Fine. They are offers you can refuse.

Right after WTC, I was approached with all kinds of offers: TV commercials, endorsements, PP dolls, even high-wire-walks with me dressed like a hamburger to launch some fast-food franchise. It was easy for me to send them all to hell.

I was not about to use my art to sell products (the national sport of my country of adoption); in fact, the more zeroes the hungry promoters added to the sums they were offering, the angrier I became.

With the savvy of a street urchin, however, I avoided saying no outright. Instead, I would glance at my blank date book and declare, "I'm totally booked this month . . . Oh, wait! At the beginning of next week I might be able to squeeze in a lunch or dinner." And just like that, I ended up eating twice a day at the best restaurants in town. With vicious satisfaction, I soon learned to conceal my contempt for the despicable deals until *after* I had ordered my third dessert.

Don't hunger to be recognized. But if you become famous, you will notice how the instruments you were missing to open certain doors can be provided by *Celebrity*. Use its powers judiciously to chart your progress, but be aware it is a highly ephemeral commodity.

And be forewarned, as I was able to warn myself: the pause you take to marvel at your own success may end up being of infinite duration. Let your curiosity generate impatience: remain on the move and move on.

What's next?

"How can you top what you did?" is a trick question.

My answer is to question the question with another question: "Are you tempted to raise a golden ox on the altar of facility and genuflect in worship; or are you possessed by truth and depth enough to reveal and hold on to the essence of who you should be, or perhaps who you are?"

The first choice is a form of intellectual suicide. The second, a vow of interminable hardship that comes with immeasurable joys!

I ask you, but ask yourself:

"Was there anything missing during your struggle to achieve your 'masterpiece'? Anything that could have made the fight more effective?"

Wouldn't the most satisfying reply be "No, nothing"?

And regarding the outcome, the coup itself, if I ask:

"If you would do again what you just did, that is, *what could not be done*, would you change anything for the coup to be more . . . well, perfect?" What would the answer be?

Even after forty years, my WTC performance—which feels to me as if it happened yesterday—yields a hefty collection of *if*s, from which I'll pull only one:

If minutes before the walk, at the time I was putting on my costume, I had not accidentally thrown into the void my black turtleneck—to this day if and how that happened remains a mystery—I would not have been forced to wear a gray undershirt that prevented my silhouette from looking exactly the same as my street-juggling character, which had been one of my most fervent wishes associated with the coup!

Following the performance of a tour de force, "the next step" proves too simple a concept. The post-miracle notion of *next* undoubtedly calls for a myriad of steps; I am talking here about the art of walking, which implies a direction if not a destination.

Therefore, consider your life so far and ponder its evolution: lean on the past-present (a tense I made up, about the only one that make sense to me) to decide your future-perfect.

The question that counts is "What's missing in your life?"—creativity-wise, of course.

Invent the horizon of an answer!

Good old "new"

Think up new targets.

Set new "crimes" in motion.

Go back to doing your homework.

Construct a new *Cathedral of Creativity*. And, of course, stake the joint!

Make new plans.

Work the details.

Practice and rehearse.

If caught . . . escape!

Execute the new coup and embrace its consequences.

Five. Like the fingers on my hand. In the above paragraph I used "new" five times.

We are used to this shiny little adjective, but do not let yourself be fooled by its innocent appearance; it is anything but.

The dangers of NEW are plentiful.

To be first makes glorious sense if you are running a marathon. But in the gallop of creativity, it is absurd to aim at being, say, "the first inventor" of a motivation cogwheel.

I assure you, the creative energy you spend beating time and distance at their own games will not be directed to the fulfillment of your quest.

Stay clear of competing—even against yourself. (Don't even think about gluing little white rings to the frames of mirrors!)

Instead, devote your resources to the pursuit of novel creations by evolving.

Nathalie Enterline, Francis Brunn's longtime partner and stage-assistant, is a performing artist with a unique act that combines dance, baton-twirling and hat-juggling. She used to begin her performance with a spot-on Chaplin impersonation, complete with mustache, black baggy pants, cane and bowler hat. Recently, she came up with a radically different presentation. She starts her act with a mischievous dance in a gray costume, evoking Chaplin with a few snatches of his classic tunes and characteristic moves much more vividly than any impersonation could.

Recapture the naive spirit of new-for-the-first-time. Do you remember, at the dawn of childhood, first being able to do things without help or guidance— walk five steps forward, bring a spoonful of soup to your mouth, utter a complete sentence, turn a doorknob? For me, these firsts felt like intimate victories, conquests tinted by a fresh, pure dye. This new was immensely rewarding: it proved my progress, reinforced my beliefs, empowered my explorations and inspired me to multiply my attempts. As I grew up, because I preserved that spirit of the new (and that innocence), I was able to embark upon larger-than-life goals, unaware they were impossible!

Refuse to diverge from your goals in hope of establishing world records. (What are they but vain testimonies to man's longing for classification and immortality?)

The irony is not lost on me that while I never install my high wire to be the highest or the longest, nonetheless my walks end up being logged in those books of records I so despise!

And then, there is the "*new* for the sake of being new": another misleading and ill-oriented concept.

We live in a time when the illusory need to think, to find, to do something new brainwashes us. It is presented as a distinctive spice—except it has no taste.

In the meantime, we're reminded left and right that "nothing is new" (which I half believe).

I find this urge to attempt the "yet unattempted" fit for fools and quite shallow. It is too easy.

A Festival of Facility

Am I the only one to notice how some children seem naturally inclined to draw birds "facing them" and with symmetrically horizontal flight stability—that is, with their wings straight out to both sides?

And that's saying nothing about the flat-based clouds with scalloped crowns!

What about a pedestrian painter who always depicts leaves from the most recognized angle, "facing the paintbrush"? Haven't the eyes of that person ever delighted in the ever-changing shapes of foliage that nature offers?

The lack of imagination in sketching birds or clouds, as described above, is triggered by the coaching of adults eager (consciously or not) to promulgate age-old conventions. But these children are in danger of growing up to be the pedestrian painter. They are under the influence of . . . *a Festival of Facility!*

Once, I asked nine-and-a-half-year-old Gypsy, "Should a house always be drawn with one door, two windows, and the mandatory smoking chimney?" ("Leading the witness," a lawyer would object at this point.) Gypsy's answer—in her inimitable teasin'-tauntin' way—was to wink like Marilyn Monroe and keep her eyes glued to mine instead of looking at what she was drawing: a large, elegant teepee . . . and conclude by slamming her pencil in satisfaction on the table (like one of those Bavarian beer drinkers of yester-chapter)!

Fight conventions!

Fight facility!

This is why I prefer never to utter the words "I love you."

First, their plainness dilutes the profound feeling of fondness. I'd certainly feel offended if you addressed your esteem and attachment to me in those barely attired terms; doesn't our relationship deserve a better-dressed expression?

Second, "I love you" are not your words! They belong to millions of people before you. Why borrow such a hackneyed expression dulled by universal habit?

Choose a more personal verbal assembly—something that expresses your personality or, more to the point, your complex appreciation for the one you love.

If I were a screenwriter, I would come up with something like "It warms my heart when you glance at me from the corner of your smile." Or "Your asymmetrical way of shuffling toward the bed is beyond sexy!"

Make yourself uncomfortable

I tell you what. Now that we have had the world at our feet, it is time to refuse complacency! Let's not sit back in the depth of the plush armchair of success: let's not adopt a comfortable system.

Actually, quite the opposite, let's make ourselves deliberately uncomfortable!

Let's, like . . . try things—totally! (I'm saying hello to some of my teenage readers.)

Experimentation should be your next experiment.

Once more, follow your intuition—but not necessarily with logic as your tour guide.

Once, in a deserted art gallery, I juggled to the sound of a painting. (I have a photograph to prove it!)

Force yourself to pay attention to boring objects, even to those common household items we see and walk by every day.

Inside the most ordinary objects hide the richest creative opportunities, waiting to be awakened. As one kid discovered, an empty washing machine transformed into a set of drums!*

Make yourself uncomfortable, I insist!

Be interested in what disturbs you.

Rebel against your own inclinations. You love classical music? Put on some heavy metal!

*http://www.wimp.com/boydrums/.

Be guided by *wabi-sabi*, a Japanese aesthetic that finds beauty in imperfection and in the cycles of nature, including growth, decay and death.

Interrupt yourself. As I do, writing, whenever the butterfly of daydreaming flutters too close to my cheeks. Don't be shy, be bold.

By reading spy novels, we learn this little-known maneuver.

If you're being followed on the sidewalk by two secret agents (and if you're a spy worth your pint of invisible ink, you'll know you're *being tailed*), the classic reaction is to cross the street hastily, stop in front of a store window, and use its reflection to identify who's following you (the *tails*). But far more effective is this lesser-known defense strategy: make an abrupt U-turn and walk straight at the *tails*! If they are less than first-class, you might catch a glimpse of their surprise or their temporary confusion. If they're really good, they'll pass you by and continue on as if nothing has happened. Then the game is endless. You can turn around once more—you're now following the followers—and observe how they adjust their hunter's behavior now that they are the prey!

Or you might simply stop abruptly in your tracks.

These abrupt changes remind me of the quick-change artists who flourished in the vaudeville theater era but have almost disappeared today. They were expert at switching almost instantly from one impersonated character to another, a drastically different character—sometimes without the benefit of a single prop.

When was the last time you did an abrupt U-turn—in life or on your way somewhere?

No, truly, I'm asking you.

Did you ever make a sudden, unpremeditated 180-degree turn? And not because you suddenly realized you forgot your car keys!

I've never done it, but I am giving serious thought to taking a sabbatical. (I'll confess to you that I know shockingly little about sabbaticals, which to me—thanks to Goya's *Witches' Sabbath*—are evocative of some rather decadent feast of the flesh rather than the period of paid leave granted to a professor to study and travel.)

Seriously, I would be inclined to stop creating for a while if I were convinced that simply meditating on creativity would boost mine.

So bury yourself in achieving your dreams—or take a leave of absence from the doing (or even use **misdirection**!) in order to devote yourself to the pondering. It's up to you.

Now, as my reader—whether you study books or plow the earth—I must salute your balancing with me all along like a true funambulist: you did not succumb to my madness.

Maybe because, as Valance Lippovitch* once declared (in Moscow, after one chess game and lots of vodka): "There is a method to Philippe Petit's madness!"

Galaxies and constellations

At the end of my one-man show, I would point at the mobile created by sculptor and set designer extraordinaire John Kahn (who lives on Easter Island), which by then had all the props used during the performance

---

*In 1966, Russian student-journalist Valance Lippovitch (a descendant of the tsars) saved Philippe from being arrested for street-juggling in Moscow's Red Square. Lippovitch—who refuses to give any information about himself or to be photographed other than from behind—became Philippe's biggest fan and vowed to follow the artist's every move from then on. Philippe adamantly said, "Hell, no!" but then his other side said, "Why not?" To this day, Philippe continues to grant episodic "exclusive" interviews to Lippovitch.

suspended in midair and twirling in slow motion over the audience. And I would conclude: "If I were a galaxy, this would be my constellation!"

But today I do not gesture from the stage, I point at the finished manuscript.

In parting, I could throw a "Bon voyage" at you. But wouldn't that be borrowing from the *Festival of Facility*? Instead, allow me to take my leave with the otherworldly "Felicitous interstellar explorations!" and hope you'll hop from planet to planet with a sense of wonder, as they are as numerous as grains of sand on a very large beach. (Does that make you dizzy? It does me.)

"May you be one of the many, many sole survivors (soul survivors) of my creative odyssey!"

I wanted to end this book with an ellipsis, but William Blake just dropped in. "The fool who persists in his folly will become wise."

But wait, I'm the author of this book, and I demand the last word! Actually, it is a word that somehow managed to slip through the net of this book; I leave it here for you to embrace:

PERSEVERANCE

(((((((((((((((**misdirection**)))))))))))))))

Improvisation needs help sometimes. That's why magicians, pickpockets and con men invented misdirection, or so it seems.

What is misdirection?

Look here:

One of my first memories from school is of a breezeless June afternoon with all the classroom windows opened in an absurd attempt to expel the heat as the urge to daydream blocked any teaching from reaching me.

Looking around, I saw that my neighbor's pencil had an eraser; mine had none. I could have grabbed the coveted item with brute force, be called a thief, and be caught red-handed. Instead, I pointed at the sky outside and screamed, "It's snowing!"

A human reflex had everyone in the room (including the nun-teacher) look outside for one second before they realized the absurdity of the information—and turned back to the classroom to try to catch the prankster. Too late!

The teaching resumed, but my neighbor was reprimanded several times because he kept looking around and under his desk for his beautiful pencil—which, alas, had been lost forever. (I still have it—Patrick Pinloche, if you read this, call me, I'll give it back to you.)

Once, running with a friend up the staircase of one tower to scout the roof of WTC, we heard a guard with his walkie-talkie on the next landing. But we could not turn around and head down because we heard people climbing up below us.

Unable to warn my friend—or myself—I dived into a loud argument with him as we kept climbing. He fell in with my acting and my body language. Absorbed in our raging exchange, hands flying right and left, we brushed by the guard, ignoring his presence!

Misdirection can move mountains. Certainly it can render large objects invisible.

A couple of years ago, after a lecture at Yale University, as I was exploring the grounds, I noticed an outdoor festival of creativity for children in full swing. I opted for the most crowded attraction, sitting on the grass and waiting with kids and parents.

The master of ceremonies was a young woman dressed as a farmer from the Outback (the show was fresh from Australia*) in a wide-brim canvas hat complete with dangling corks to repel the flies. She explained in her colorful accent that she would be presenting to the audience "live prehistoric animals" in order of size, from the smallest to the largest. She disappeared through an opening in the large curtain to the right and reappeared a second later cradling in her arms an adorable baby *Triceratops*. Endearing reaction from the audience.

A few more dinosaurs—actually, very well-made puppets—followed, growing larger and larger, some with articulated limbs and turning heads, to the delight of the kids.

Then she gave a lengthy introduction to the star of the show: "His Majesty, the most enormous, most vociferous, the deadliest and cruel . . . *T. rex!*" The kids screamed with glee, some of them with terror.

She went through the door, and a moment passed. Then she reappeared with a frown of apology: "I'm so sorry, *T. rex* refuses to come out. He might not be feeling so well . . . Hold on, let me see if I can convince him." And once again she went offstage. As we strained to hear the soft conversation in the wings, everyone—including me, a misdirection specialist!—kept our eyes riveted to the opening in the curtain. And then we all screamed, shaken out of our trance by the appearance of a fifteen-foot *T. rex*, spitting fire and violently shaking his tail until it almost brushed the front row! The giant puppet had been onstage for a few seconds, but no one had noticed its entrance from the opposite side of the little door, stage left. I applauded the clever "festival of misdirection"—as bold as any I'd ever dreamed up on a sultry June afternoon.

Misdirection can move your mountains!
Try it at home.

*"Erth Dinosaur Petting Zoo" was created and performed by Erth Visual & Physical Inc.

((((((((((((((((((•))))))))))))))))))

AN AFTERTHOUGHT

Conquistador of the Useless

Thank you, Werner, for saluting me with this most honorable title.*

Many of the values I deem essential in guiding my journeys—passion, imagination, intuition, observation—seem to others useless. Useless, that is, in the sense that they do not build roads and schools and hospitals. Yet they are the bread and water that allow creativity to survive.

In my early printing apprenticeship, I developed the habit of inserting the word *Uselessness* into the composing stick, with a capital U that highlighted its nobility and poetic spirit.

Circa 1800, while visiting Rome, the writer Stendhal was accosted by an American tourist (rare at the time) who pointed at the monumental dome of St. Peter's and asked:

"What's the use of that?"

"It's for making our heart beat, when we see it from afar!" replied the writer.

---

*His full statement, which appears on the back of *On the High Wire*, ends, "I salute you, Philippe, the Fragile Man of the Wire, the Emperor of the Air. Like Fitzcarraldo you are one of the ever so rare and wondrous men: a Conquistador of the Useless. I bow my head in reverence."

Talking about heartbeats: One day the sculptor John Kahn offered Kathy and me the gift of "eternal invisible mobility." He pinned to the wall of our living room a small magnet, and about twelve inches below it, a sewing needle suspended from a length of thread. When he brought the needle into proximity with the magnet, it was immediately held in a vertical position in midair—like magic. If you look closely, you can see the needle oscillating minutely, constantly freeing itself and becoming prisoner of the attraction.

Similarly, we should try to hold ourselves prisoner of the magnetism of our passion, so that our creative forces never cease to vibrate.

I would like to leave you with some aphorisms I have chosen for you in parting, in lieu of advice and commandments, written on little orange index-cards that I was just going to lay out on this large sheet of white Bristol when I was interrupted . . .

What happened?

I was suddenly whisked far away by the music I was listening to while scribbling.

Unbeknownst to me, my hand hung suspended above the little cards until I noticed the golden nib hovering, softly dancing to the concluding phrases of Bach's Fugue No. 24 in B minor from Book I of *The Well-Tempered Clavier*, as played by my friend Evelyne Crochet.*

And then, after a beat of silence, from Schubert's *Three Piano Pieces, Opus Posthumous*, came the Allegro assai of No. 1 in E-flat minor.

The dissimilitude of the two kinds of magnificence was a delight to my ears, Bach's thoughtful *au-revoir* followed by Schubert's exultant *bonjour*.

Evelyne Crochet Plays Bach, Schubert, Satie. Excerpts taken from the following recordings:
Bach: Music & Arts CD-1180 (4); Schubert: Philips LP S900-178; Satie: Philips LP S900-179.

The pianist at her Steinway grand has again displayed her pure and immense talent, pulling me away to reverie, taking me by inspiration, reminding me once more that vulnerability can be a force in the most demanding of arts.

In case you're wondering, I never ask music to provide a background to the picture I'm painting. I do not write and listen to music. I write *with* the music, as a dancer set in motion by music is compelled to keep moving because of it.

Music is my accomplice. In the same way it invited me to suspend my writing, it now whispers to me to return to the orange index-cards.

Where was I?

Oh yes.

With Schubert still watching over my shoulder, I move the cards around, like a close-up magician performing an undetectable *false shuffle*, until I arrive at the order in which I wish them to appear on the page. But then another interruption, of the daydreaming kind, guides my fingers to absentmindedly assemble the cards into an image . . . Look!—no misdirection here—I've built two towers!

Between the towers' rooftops, I quickly add my aerial signature: the hieroglyph of a tiny wirewalker on a smiling catenary curve. And I muse at another Useless notion: how to make my first step poetically visible. I extend one leg in slow motion. I bring one foot with toes pointed delicately in contact with the steel cable. I suspend my breath in order to shift my weight with control of balance. I give my other foot to the cable.

That's but one of the infinite ways I can share with the audience that—on the wire as well as in life—a first step is a point of no return.

Back to work I now share with you my comments:

Welcome interruptions. Take advantage of them. They are there to enrich your creativity.

But your curiosity has been teased long enough: here is what's written on the cards:

Cards of advice

Learn languages and travel—not necessarily in that order.

Those who want to achieve something find a way; those who do not, an excuse.

Disorder and chaos will serve you as long as you direct them. Experience the *School of Hard Knocks*.

We should be interested in what disturbs us: cultivate contradictions.

Let's observe how nature inspires.

Develop unabashedly your own set of morals, cling to your own logic, inhabit your own universe: teach yourself as you let life teach you.

Learn and teach, teach and learn. Who dares to teach must never cease to learn.

Choose your teachers, choose your students.

Pass on your secrets before they die of neglect.

If you don't know what the rules are, it is easier to break them.

If you feel you have no choice, you're probably heading in the right direction.

Cultivate elas*tiiiiii*city, expand.

Let your tools lilt; your soul will dance.

Place the creative act—not its attainment—in your heart. The wire-walker intent on safety deprives the onlookers of aerial poetry.

When Perfection seduces you, give yourself to her embrace.

In Greek, *enthousiasmos* means to be possessed by the gods. Do not let them relinquish you.

For transition, I'll borrow from my friend Robert Doisneau, the witty photographer: "Forgive quickly, kiss slowly."

Cards to live by

Practice stubbornness. Arrogance is fine as long as you earn it.

Go to extremes to shelter your creative process from negative influences.

Do not specialize. Do it all.

Do not run away from the perils of perfection! Polish your work like a stone that passes through many hands.

Do not leave anything to chance; chance is a thief that never gets caught.

Prove yourself every day. Reject comfort and security; rebel against the unpoetic.

Sharpen your intellectual paranoia: remember to suspect—question the question!

Practice the dismemberment of the expected.

Become the castaway on the Easter Island of your dreams!

And here, an ultimate interruption—from the heart—commands me to take pen and Wite-Out and let the little man on the wire further explore the azure . . . I draw a hot-air balloon above the wire-walker and then I white him out—he, I, just climbed into the balloon's gondola.

I disappear into the clouds like Cosimo Piovasco di Rondò in Italo Calvino's *The Baron in the Trees.*

No one, not even me, will ever find out whether I surrender to the caprice of the winds or deftly take advantage of the air currents and the changes in temperature to guide the air vessel into the territory of my dreams . . .

Philippe Petit
June 17, 2013

In my secret office in the Triforium Gallery of the Cathedral Church of Saint John the Divine—where I have been Artist-in-Residence since 1980—on the anniversary of my little Cordia-Gypsy's birth.*

*The ashes of Cordia-Gypsy Fasula/Petit (1982–1992) rest in the cathedral's columbarium, a peaceful harbor I urge you to visit. If you do, find Gypsy and throw a smile—with the swiftness of a juggler, she'll surely catch it.

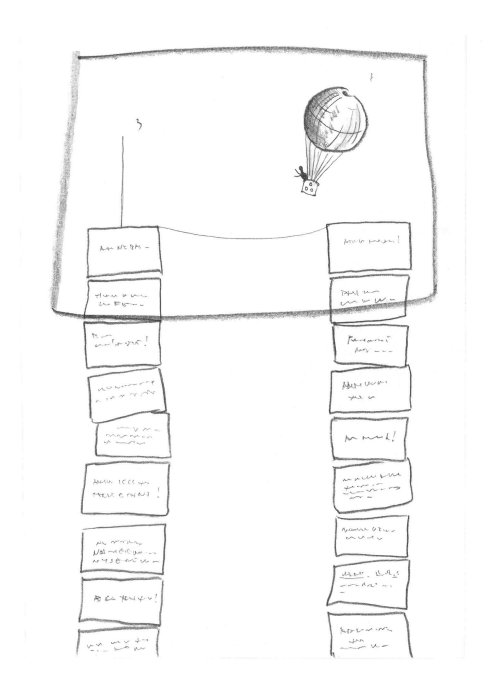

Acknowledgments

My editor, Becky Saletan (led by my childish but respectful habit of being proprietary about things and people, I was about to write "my Becky"!), was instrumental in driving toward fruition the project of a book. "It should not be a book about creativity in general," she reminded me, "but a book about *your* creativity." I praise her for her vision and thank her for her collaboration and expertise.

The writer Marshall Messer* suggested the book's fitting title and subtitle. To embrace it in full, I came up with a chapter progression that mirrored the preparations for a bank robbery or, in my case, an illegal high-wire walk.

Then a dear accomplice helped immensely. That accomplice is, as always, Kathy O'Donnell, my Partner-in-Crime, Confederate Co-Conspirator and Producer for more than twenty-five years. She took command in supporting me and this project unequivocally. Her contributions are always generous as well as to the point, her criticisms are always constructive as well as acute; that's why she is always the first person to read my first drafts. Thank you, *my* KOD.

*Marshall Messer, *Change at Jamaica* (New York: BMA Press, 2013).

RIVERHEAD BOOKS

An imprint of Penguin Random House LLC

375 Hudson Street

New York, New York 10014

The author gratefully acknowledges permission to quote from the following:

"Palabras para Julia" in *Palabras para Julia* by José Agustín Goytisolo.

© Herederos de José Agustín Goytisolo.

"Come to the Edge" by Christopher Logue. Copyright © Christopher Logue, 1996.

The Library of Congress has catalogued the Riverhead hardcover edition as follows:

Petit, Philippe, date.

Creativity : the perfect crime / Philippe Petit.

p.   cm.

ISBN 978-1-59463-168-9

1. Creation (Literary, artistic, etc.).   2. Creative ability.   I. Title.

PN56.C69P54   2014   2014000484

801'.92—dc23

Riverhead hardcover edition: May 2014

Riverhead trade paperback edition: August 2015

Riverhead trade paperback ISBN: 978-1-59463-387-4

Printed in the United States of America

1   3   5   7   9   10   8   6   4   2

BOOK DESIGN BY CLAIRE NAYLON VACCARO

FROM AN ORIGINAL CONCEPT BY THE AUTHOR